The Adventurous Bowmen

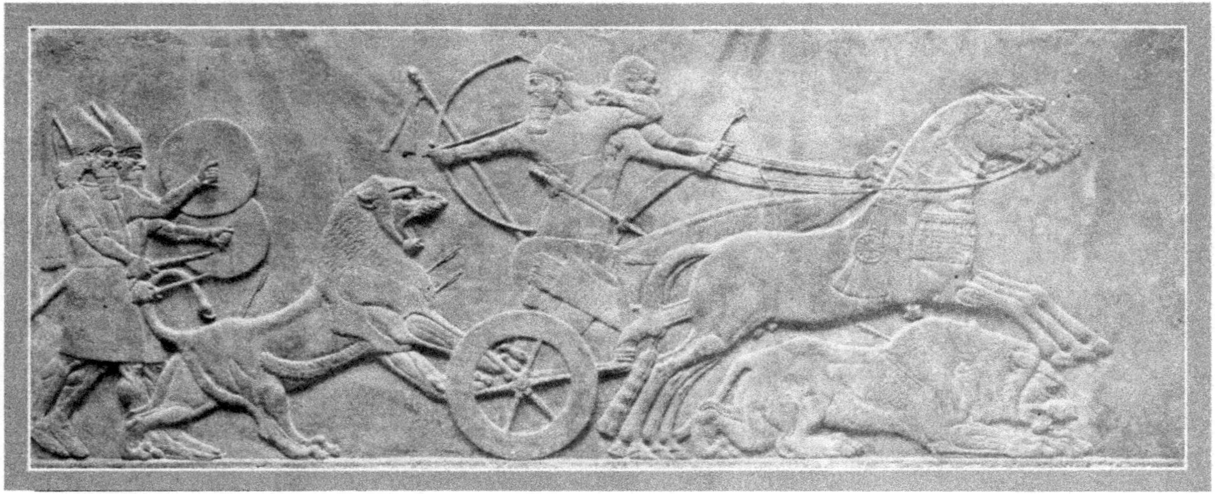

AN ASSYRIAN LION HUNT

THE Adventurous Bowmen

FIELD NOTES ON AFRICAN ARCHERY

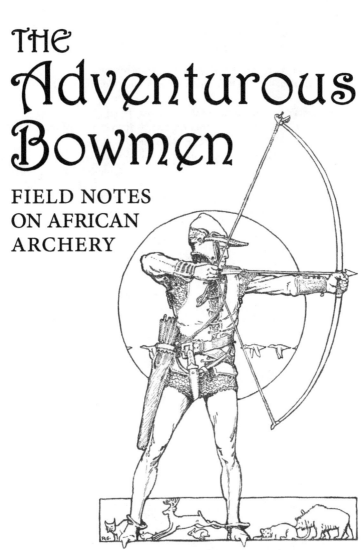

Saxton Pope

COMMONWEALTH BOOK COMPANY
St. Martin, Ohio
2024

ISBN (paperback) 978-1-948986-81-6
ISBN (hardcover) 978-1-948986-82-3

CONTENTS

CONTENTS

ILLUSTRATIONS

ILLUSTRATIONS

THE ADVENTUROUS BOWMEN

The Adventurous Bowmen

I

A PROLOGUE IN MOMBASA

April 7th, 1925.

HUNTING is a primitive instinct and had its origin in the early life of man, when he evolved from a purely vegetarian existence and added grubs, bugs, small mammals, crustaceans and birds to his diet.

From a defensive attitude toward the larger animals, man took on one of assault and found the food problem correspondingly more to his taste.

So with all elemental people today, we find that food is the first big issue of their lives and that the hunter is a person of importance in the community.

Man has made his conquest of the world directly through his weapons of the chase. With the bow and the spear, he has not only held his own against the stronger beasts of the forest and plains, but he has·put them to rout and usurped the earth.

The plowshare has followed the hunter, and habitation anywhere beyond his arboreal refuge has been made possible only by his weapons. The hunter is not to be taken lightly, nor has his spirit vanished from the land. There is in the heart of every man the impulse of the chase. It is, of course, developed in some natures more intensely than in others. Even in the tribal stage, individuals were marked by one prominent gift or another: there were musicians, artisans, medicine men, warriors and hunters.

We cannot expect, therefore, that every man should have the same quantitative urge, but the hunting spirit is normal and laudable, and so long as there is game to be taken so long will the hunter follow the quest.

We who live in America, a country still wild in large areas, are privileged to hunt freely. Game abounds in many places and protective laws will preserve it for years to come.

In California, where the densely forested Sierra Nevada and Coast Range mountains present ideal game retreats for deer, panther and bear, we can hunt to our heart's content. Though this is an age of accurate ballistics and high explosives, a small group of men out west have taken up the use of the old English long bow as a weapon of the chase, and prefer to drive a clothyard shaft at a running deer than to lay him low with a bullet.

This return to the pastime and pursuits of our ancestors, is more sport and has a halo of romance.

Therefore we have gone out into the forest solitudes and upland pastures armed only with the bow and arrow. And though we have in no way been competitors with those who shoot guns, though we admittedly are greatly inferior in our capacity to bring meat into camp, we have had a much greater satisfaction.

The man who shoots with the bow must put his strength of arm into his weapon. His eye must be clear and his nerve steady. He must approach his game by greater skill than if he used a rifle.

Hunting becomes more a contest of cunning between the beast and the man, and the factors are more equal than if the man were armed with that implement of destruction and precision, the high power rifle.

We have hunted for more than ten years with the bow, and our bag has included all the small game of the land, such as quail, ducks, geese, grouse, squirrels· and rabbits. We have also shot deer in goodly number, more than a dozen bear, including grizzly and the great Alaskan bear. We have killed cougars and moose and mountain sheep. Our record for American big game is filled out and stands as an everlasting credit to our beloved weapon.

This should have satisfied us; we have done what our forefathers have done, no more could be asked, but friends came to us and spoke of other worlds to conquer.

Stewart Edward White, a writer, who spent some months hunting in Africa, became interested in archery

5

and later suggested that we try our artillery on the beasts of this tropical country. He says that he has no further desire to shoot them with the gun.

Then Leslie Simson invited us to visit him in his camp in Tanganyika. He is an American mining engineer who made a competence in Johannesburg, and decided to take a vacation. He has spent the last twenty years taking a complete rest, shooting lions, elephants and other specimens of this sort for sport and the various museums.

We accepted his cordial offer and included in our party Mr. Arthur Young, a young Californian, who is an expert rifle shot, as well as a good bowman. We have hunted much together. He recently spent two years in Alaska taking moving pictures of the landscape and wild life. Some of these films depict him shooting moose, mountain sheep and kadiak bear with the bow and arrow.

We three laid our plans to join Simson in Tanganyika.

In the past ages other men have pursued African game with the bow and arrow. Every great Egyptian ruler seems to have on his tomb a record of his hunting exploits. There we see birds, jackals, gazelles and lions pierced by arrows. The Assyrian Kings hunted lions in Northern Syria; Assur Nasir-Pal shows us in bas-relief a picture of his hunting experiences. He shoots from a racing chariot; beaters drive lions out of the jungle; arrow slain beasts lie on the ground about him; it is a royal hunt.

Other rock engravings depict the king grasping a lion by the throat and stabbing him with a short sword. The beast is full of arrows and this probably is the death stroke. We have no reason to doubt the courage of the king, but there is a suggestion of dramatic license here.

At least there is every evidence to prove that archers have invaded Africa long before our day. And, of course, we know there are millions of natives who use the bow and arrow in the wilds of Ethiopia today as they have for thousands of years in the past.

But since the epoch of the Crusades, no archers shooting the English long bow and the broadhead arrow have been in the country, and never to our knowledge has any representative of Robin Hood's Merrie Men ever loosed a flying shaft in that continent of mighty beasts. It was therefore with a profound feeling of the romantic significance of the event that we planned to carry the legend of the long bow into the jungles of Africa. We were to journey to the last stronghold of big game; we were to make a holy pilgrimage to the Mecca of all mighty hunters; we had set ourselves the task of vindicating the honor of the arms of our English forefathers with the yew long bow and the broadhead arrow.

As in days of old, each archer makes his own tackle.

7

We construct our bows of California yew. We make our shafts, feather them and head them ourselves. How this is done, how we have revived the ancient craft of the bowyer and fletcher is a long story and told in the book *Hunting with the Bow and Arrow*, to which, as the author, I refer you, with sly satisfaction. The publisher, let me say, is the same as he who prints this volume: one Putnam's Sons, No. 2 West 45th Street, New York City; with this gentle hint I leave you to read on.

So we gathered our equipment together; tropical clothes and boots, personal belongings and surgical supplies, for you must know I am a doctor of medicine, and then our archery tackle.

This last consists of some half dozen bows apiece, carried in a cylindrical case made of light paper composition and an arrow box of similar tough material, in which each archer carries a hundred or more arrows, lying on little racks, to hold them apart.

Besides this outfit we have in our baggage, arrow shafts, feathers and steel arrowheads sufficient for two thousand more arrows, with all the glue and silk ribbon, paint and other requisites for the manufacture of these missiles.

No one knows how much ammunition we need, so we have an abundance. Our bows are made of yew wood or osage orange. Their length is five feet six or eight inches and each one pulls from sixty to ninety pounds

8

when the arrow is full drawn. The strings are made of Irish linen, well waxed.

The arrow shafts are of birch, three-eighths of an inch in diameter and twenty-eight inches in length. We feather them with pinions from the turkey, glued and bound on with silk. The points of the arrows are made of steel blades three inches long by one and a quarter inches wide, riveted in a tubular steel haft or socket in which the arrow shaft is set with ferule cement.

Such a missile can be shot about two hundred yards and will penetrate an animal the size of a deer as far off as it can hit him. Driven at shorter ranges our arrows have often gone completely through these animals even after severing ribs and other large bones. Lighter shafts can be shot nearly three hundred yards. Arrows kill by hemorrhage, they have no power to produce shock or to shatter a bone. They can kill an animal as quickly and humanely as a rifle ball.

The accuracy of our weapon is, of course, greatly inferior to that of a modern gun. When shot side by side, the bow seems a crude haphazard implement and suffers by comparison. But in spite of this disparity the bow and arrow in the hands of a trained archer does have a degree of precision all its own, one that can be controlled and is surprising to the uninitiated.

Roughly speaking this is what the bow is capable of doing. Shooting at the standard target having a nine-inch bull's eye, at forty yards, a good archer will strike the central circle with the majority of his arrows. At one hundred yards he will hit this same bull's eye once in six times and place most of his arrows in a four foot target. Shooting at game, he should hit an animal the size of a quail or rabbit at twenty yards nearly every shot. A deer at sixty or eighty yards he should strike with one of three arrows and a deer will often stand and let one shoot this number of shots. We have even killed running deer at this distance.

Larger flights are more a matter of chance, but Will Compton broke the neck of an antelope at one hundred and ten yards, Monte, the Indian, hit a deer in the forehead at ninety yards and dropped it in its tracks, the arrow emerging through the neck.

But we try as a rule to approach animals of this size to a distance less than fifty yards, where we are fairly certain of striking them in a vital spot and dispatching them quickly.

So, having outfitted ourselves with all things necessary for a prolonged stay in the tropics, besides our artillery, and having arranged in advance with the firm Safariland, Ltd. to supply us with men, food and all other necessities while in British East Africa, we set forth in February, 1925.

After crossing the continent we sailed from New York on the White Star Line, March 6th, bound for Cherbourg, France. We crossed France and after a few days sailed again from Marseilles, passing through the Mediterranean, the Suez Canal, down the Red Sea and the Indian Ocean.

This part of the voyage required nearly three weeks and we spent our time in reading, exercising, playing music and making archery tackle. The weather was pleasant throughout and on April 6th we sailed into the harbor of Kilindini and disembarked at the town of Mombasa.

This is an ancient Portuguese fortified town, and long a bone of contention between contending nations. Its name signifies the "Island of Wars." The old fortifications of 400 years, built by Vasco Da Gama, still guard the harbor and bear witness to many bloody episodes of the past. Here for the first time we get the real flavor of Africa. The first thing you notice upon sailing into the harbor is that the breeze from off the green, palm beaches, is as fragrant as spice. It smells like Chinese matting in which delicate incense has been rolled. It is a most surprising phenomenon!

We were landed by swarms of handsome black boys in picturesque, gaudy rags, and carried safely to shore in their small boats. The whole scene is strangely interesting, in spite of the ubiquitous Ford automobile that chugs past. One is struck immediately by the fact that man power is the motive element of the country. Trucks or wagons are used to haul baggage, or loads of sand, or building material, but men pull and push them; no horses are in evidence. Heavy loads are carried on the backs of small black men, whose stature in no way suggests the strength that lies in thigh and shoulders. These Swahili are a handsome lot of natives, some dressed in the costume of the municipal police, khaki jackets, short knee pants, blue spiral puttees, red fez caps and belts; they present a comic yet engaging appearance. They are armed only with a police whistle and a short club, these and the authority of the British Government are all they need. Jinrickshas and bicycles are two more anachronisms of the place, but they also add to the strangeness of the scene.

The bows and arrows were a puzzle to the customs officials, since they could be classified neither under the head of guns, ammunition or fishing tackle, so they gave them up as an enigma, and taxed us lightly for the material used, for when we told them that we make our own tackle, they had no means of estimating their value. We found our English cousins very cordial and willing to assist us in our expedition.

From Mombasa the railroad train leaves every alternate day for Nairobi, the capital of Kenya Colony, situated more than four hundred miles inland, at an elevation of five thousand feet above sea level.

Waiting here for this final stage of our journey we begin to absorb the atmosphere of the tropics. The heat beneath the equatorial sun does not seem so oppressive as I've often felt it in some of the interior

A STREET IN MOMBASA

valleys of California, though the humidity is quite noticeable.

The multiplicity of pleasant black servants, the tropical fruits, the luxuriant vegetation, the quaint old gardens, the beautiful walks along the island sea coast, the strange Arabic architecture, the fantastic native quarters, the Mohammedan mosques and minarets, the jewelled heavens at night, the balm and spice of the air and the great calm that rests upon the place make Mombasa a city of Magic.

If this is the overture to our African adventure, then let what is to follow come in such measure as the Gods appoint. We lean forward with eager delight.

II

WE ARRIVE IN TANGANYIKA

April 14th, 1925.

HERE we are in Tanganyika, the most distant possible point from our home in San Francisco; twelve hours ahead of the sunset in the Golden Gate.

We arrived yesterday in the permanent camp of Leslie Simson, on the Sironera river. This is a place some two hundred and forty miles south of Nairobi, in what was once German East Africa. The journey used to take a month by foot safari. We started four days ago from Nairobi in three automobiles. With us we took the better part of our equipment and seven natives as tent boys and gun bearers. I say gun bearers provisionally, because those boys are to carry archery equipment and not guns.

When we told Leslie Tarlton, whose outfitting firm supplies men for safaris, that we wanted boys to carry arrows for a hunting party, he had some difficulty in getting volunteers. A gun boy takes a big enough chance as it is with the average sportsman and the

14

average African lion. They could not see the faintest possible chance of coming home safely after an encounter where the hunter was armed only with a bow and arrow.

But when it was explained to them that we would also employ native spearmen, and after they examined our powerful bows and broadhead arrows and saw how we shot them, we secured two Wakamba and one Swahili, who were familiar with the bow since boyhood. We intend showing these boys how to make tackle, and arm them with spears.

Two tent boys also joined our party, in addition to those in the employ of Leslie Simson.

So, having loaded our duffle in the light motor trucks, we left Nairobi on the overland trip south. Our route led through the Kadong Valley, the Thirst Valley and up on the high escarpments which constitute the Sarangeti Plains. A part of this journey was on dirt road and some over the simple ditched track recently laid out for the Duke of York's expedition. But most of the way was over the rolling veldt, along Masai cattle trails, across dry creek beds, or dongas, around mountain slopes, and over grass covered prairies which comprise this portion of Africa.

A few years ago when some friends invited me to join them on an African hunt, I said that I did not care to go to a country of red dirt, intense heat, smelly natives, innumerable insects and diseases.

But here we found a land of astonishing verdure; every foot is covered with grass, with scattered acacia or thorn trees throughout. Flowers bloom the year round. It is a high plateau, quite temperate in the morning, evening and night, even cold then; and hot only for a few hours in the middle of the day; otherwise a great deal like the uplands of Arizona and Wyoming. And yet this country is within three hundred miles of the equator.

It was a distinct surprise and pleasure to see not only the typical African vegetation such as cocoanut palms, the thorn trees, the Euphorbia and the rank jungle growth along the streams, but also to recognize many old friends in grasses, weeds and flowers.

Some fields were ablaze with intense color: brilliant orange, golden yellow, and deep purple flowers, the latter centered beneath the shade trees; all the colors of this land are of a distinctly deeper tone than in our country.

In some places where the automobiles drove through long grass, a sweet fragrance arose, as if aromatic herbs were crushed and gave forth their perfume: most astonishing and delightful!

As we traveled we passed native villages, mostly in the Masai Reserve where curious spectators ran forth to see us, for the flivver is still a marvelous apparition in their eyes. At difficult spots on the road, or where broken bridges necessitated a rough detour, we had the assistance of these Masai in dragging us out with ropes. These handsome, fearless men, with their inseparable spears, their beautiful statuesque bodies and their bold eyes, are good to look upon.

When we showed them our powerful bows and let them try to draw them, the first evidence of any condescension appeared in their faces. They had a little respect for the white man thus armed. Like the African lion, they are haughty and unconquered children of the jungle.

Within the last few years there have been several Masai uprisings that required machine guns to quell. Later on we hope to use their courage to back us up in some of our more dangerous hunting.

Our first night was spent at a dry camp, and we depended on tanks of water carried on the running board of the car. Here we heard for the first time the midnight roar of a wild lion. It sounded like peals of distant thunder. It did not concern us much, because we had two of the most redoubtable lion hunters in the world right in camp with us. Leslie Simson has killed more than one hundred and fifty-six lions by himself, and White has an enviable record for accuracy in game shooting and claims to have bagged thirty-six of these beasts.

As on all camping trips, much of the conversation was devoted to stirring tales of adventure or critical situations. The lion's roar led to the relation of one or two cheering episodes. Simson was speaking of lions he had met, and told of one that entered his camp, made a tremendous leap and landed at the foot of his cot, but before Simson could untangle himself from his mosquito net and drag his automatic pistol into action, the lion seized the cook who lay near and disappeared in the jungle. Search was futile, and next morning all that was found remaining were the finger nails of his faithful servant.

Several other man-eating stories told by Simson and White simply added a comforting note to the occasion. To those who wish to get the pure unadulterated "man-eating" thrill, let me recommend reading the book by Captain Patterson entitled *The Man Eaters of Tsarvo.*

Our second day led through a country thronged with game of all sorts: kongoni, topi, Grant's gazelle, Thomson's gazelle, wildebeest, zebra galore, ostrich and giraffe, and many more. They were segregated in moderate herds and often stood within a distance of a hundred yards and watched the machines go by.

It is safe to say we saw no fewer than five thousand head of game in that one day. Bands of this numbers no longer inhabit similar areas of Kenya Colony to the north, because of repeated hunting, the introduction of motor cars and the farming which has occupied the land. They have moved away. But Tanganyika will be the huntsman's paradise for many years.

We did no hunting, because the rainy season is due

and we wished to make all haste. Travel during wet weather increases the difficulties ten-fold.

At Narok in the Masai Reserve, there is now a military post. The commanding officer is Captain Horn, and the present commissioner is Captain Deck, both the finest type of English officials. They have a detachment of King's African Rifles, composed largely of the sons of Sudanese chieftains. The natty black soldier that was on guard as we drove up was a splendid specimen of manhood; dressed in his blue sweater, khaki shorts, blue spiral puttees, red fez cap and automobile tire sandals, he was a sight for the gods. Yes, the automobile tire has invaded Africa, and one is likely to see on the wild game trails a clear cut track marked "non-skid" or "nobby tread." They constitute the latest style in footgear in these parts.

Our second day was closed with the sight of two magnificent lions. Just at sunset we saw these monarchs of the land standing in the deep grass, surveying a herd of zebra, picking out a juicy meal for supper. They were only moderately surprised at seeing us, but withdrew reluctantly and with great dignity. They were a glorious sight; with grace and power marked in every lithe movement; imperious and unafraid, they leisurely stepped into the forest. They were less than a hundred yards from us when first seen. Neither party was at that moment looking for trouble.

We drove on, and later saw a third lion at forty

yards. He felt our intrusion a little more keenly and skulked into a thicket waiting for our first move. We moved on.

We also saw three cheetahs on the third day and took one on, just to show our boys what the arrows would do. We stalked him on an open plain; Simson hit him with a running shot in the leg, at eighty yards, and Young struck him at the root of the tail with an arrow. He made off, but they are easily discouraged, so we took after him on foot and ran him to a standstill, where another shot with the rifle brought him down and I finished him with two arrows, one through the neck, the other in the chest.

White declined to shoot at this animal with his rifle but handed it to Simson. He said he had no desire to do any shooting, he had enough of that in the past. He came to Africa to use the bow.

There was no particular achievement about this cheetah episode, and we did not count him as a bow and arrow trophy, but we wet our arrows to show the safari what to expect in a larger way later on.

An amusing aftermath occurred as we were through with the skinning and just about to start again. Two jackals were hanging around to join the feast, when I loosed an arrow at one some sixty yards off. The shaft seemed to strike him, but in reality it passed between his legs and as he was running it tangled him all up. It happened to be a bloody shaft that had just been

MASAI BOY AND CATTLE

used on the cheetah; the jackal, after extricating himself, seized the arrow in his teeth and ran. I quickly shot again and grazed his back, when he let fall my first arrow and galloped off over the veldt. We all had a good laugh at his expense.

Soon after this, as it began to grow dark, we neared our permanent camp and were greeted by a line of natives, happy looking boys, all attached to Simson's safari. With shining white teeth and dancing eyes they clapped their hands and shouted "Jambo Bwana!— Jambo!" and later insisted upon shaking us all gleefully by the hand.

So we have arrived, and now the camp is clothed in darkness. A dozen glowing fires burn before as many miniature grass huts; the hum of native talk fills the air. We have finished our evening meal and watch the glorious heavens of an African night.

III

OUR CAMP AND FIRST HUNT

April 17th, 1925.

SO far as can be ascertained by the maps of a country that has hardly been mapped, we lie at a point about halfway between the middle of Lake Victoria Nyanza and the volcano Kilimanjaro.

For ten years past, the surrounding country for one hundred miles has been almost the exclusive hunting grounds of Simson, one of the very few people who knows the route in and the location of water holes.

He has constructed a permanent camp near a small stream called the Sironera River, and has built there some twenty native huts. They are a picturesque collection of dwellings, with walls of wattle, composed of small sticks and mud, and the roofs of poles bound with strips of bark and reeds, thatched heavily with marsh grass.

I sit in one of these Bandas now, writing this epistle, while Simson and White have gone out on the veldt for camp meat and Arthur Young has taken his bow and sallied forth in quest of adventure.

We have finished our morning hunt and the afternoon is at our own disposal.

In camp there are about forty natives, including a headman called Mdolo, who served his apprenticeship with the famous elephant hunter Cunninghame; and a gun bearer named Kazimoto, which translated means "hot worker," for it seems that these natives give themselves advertising names descriptive of their alleged virtues.

There are besides cooks and kitchen assistants, runaway boys from the nearest village of Ikoma, thirty-five miles off; skinners, water carriers, porters, tent boys and what not. There is not a woman this side of Ikoma. Every once in a while, however, there is an urgent demand for wages among the younger natives; some mother has just died, or some dire sickness has fallen upon the victim and causes him to seek his home in Ikoma; otherwise it is a strictly masculine kingdom. We call it Simson's Principality.

We have two large huts for our own sleeping quarters and a half enclosed lounge or dining room, where we sit after meals and discuss hunting, or play music when the day is done. Apollo was a musician as well as an archer, you may recall, so like him each of us has a little stringed instrument that is small enough to be rolled up in his blankets; a violin, a mandolin, and a guitar.

In the evenings, under the stars, or by the camp

fire, we play sweet harmonies together, greatly to the delectation of our souls.

There is much formality to the service rendered by our personal servants. Our valet makes beds, provides baths, waits at table, unlaces our boots and renders other services that confuse and humiliate an American. The gun bearer, or, properly, archery bearer, besides packing an extra quiver of arrows for each of us, carries a canteen of water and a camera, chases our arrows, sharpens them with a file and in camp keeps busy cutting feathers for arrow shafts and cleaning our outfit.

Naturally there is much comedy stuff going on in a camp of this size, singing and joking among the men. Some are now preparing hides, some making dried meat. The boys, called Totos, are digging small vegetable gardens and planting garden seeds that we brought from California. But all of them are singing, and hearty negro laughter rings out on the air.

At night this is somewhat muffled up by the ghoulish, vacant laughter of the wandering hyenas, or entirely quelled for the moment by the none too distant roar of a lion.

When we first arrived, Simson asked the headman how things had progressed in his two weeks' absence. Mdolo said that none of the hyenas had come into the huts but that they had been bad, in spite of the poison. It seems that Mr. Simson's last guest was a chemist who had left a quantity of arsenic, suggesting that the cook place it in the garbage to rid the camp of these disgusting pests. This was done, but the cook reported that it only seemed to stimulate the appetites of the hyenas and improved their complexions.

When asked about Simba, or lions, the headman said they had been quite troublesome during the Bwana's absence. They chased the zebra into camp, kept up a great racket within a quarter of a mile, and two of the boys who had been sent on a journey had failed to return.

From this we were led to believe that at least these particular lions were good representative citizens.

Our first day's hunt, however, was not directed toward lions. We are not yet ready to tackle this problem. We made an official tour of Simson's domain. This was done partly in a motor car and partly on foot. This car is a light Ford truck having a canopy over the front seat and a small box body in the rear. Distant points are accessible by machine and then walking is necessary. We do not hunt from a car, because it is unsportsmanlike and, moreover, it is practically impossible to shoot a bow from any vehicle for lack of space and the necessity of a solid footing. We must do our stalking and shooting on foot.

So long as one drives a straight course across the plains it is possible to go within a hundred yards of some species of wild game. As soon, however, as it is apparent to the game that your course is one of approach, a closer range than three hundred yards is seldom permitted. If one tries to come nearer on foot, the game often retires to half a mile, where even a rifle shot would be futile.

It is certain that we cannot hunt to any extent on the open veldt, but must resort to the broken country and cover. Here we must work out our own methods of ambush and stalking.

On our first morning's hunt, we had a utilitarian object; we wanted a Thomson's gazelle for our own meat, our boys having been provided with Topi.

Herds of these beautiful little antelope are thickly interspersed among the animal multitudes that throng the open spaces. Their clean buff coats, striped lengthwise with white and black, their gracefully curved horns and necks, their trim white legs and a perpetually flickering tail, characterize them as little patricians of the veldt. They stand about two and a half feet high at the shoulder, have a chest diameter of about eight inches and are a difficult mark at any range over one hundred yards.

I was assigned the duty of shooting the first Tommy. I made one or two poor shots with the bow, then as a stroke of good fortune I succeeded in approaching within sixty yards of one and shot a clean arrow that struck him in the flanks, about six inches too far back for effective results. The arrow went through and

CAMP AT SIRONERA

out the other side of the gazelle, and with a bound he sought to join his herd.

At this moment a hyena, that had been skulking in the vicinity of the band, hoping to pick up a litle kid, took after the wounded Tommy, and attempted to run it down.

Ordinarily an animal wounded this way will lie down within a short distance if not molested. Here, however, a disturbing factor had been introduced into the chase. So we returned to our waiting car and followed the hyena. He soon perceived that he was being hunted and reluctantly gave up his quest and sought his own safety. We put on speed and started a race across the prairie. The ground was quite level, the grass short, and one had only to look out for large wart hog holes and shallow hidden ditches, and dongas.

We hit up a speed of thirty or thirty-five miles an hour and soon were at the hyena's tail as he galloped along, often turning his head, making quick dodges and trying all sorts of tricks to elude us. He purposely ran into zebra herds, through Kongoni groups, started other gazelles, both Thomson's and Grant's, in flight.

Presently we had a whole menagerie trooping across the landscape with us. Regiments of zebra ran parallel to us, antelope cut across our bows, wildebeest galloped ludicrously in and out the throng, clouds of dust arose and still we followed our hyena.

After a couple of miles running, he turned at bay and

27

out we jumped, Young and I. We shot and missed, because of our haste. The beast turned to flee again. We shot and both struck him in the back. Hindered by the arrows he ran in a large circle and we succeeded in running across this diameter and driving several more shafts through his body, when he succumbed.

We were out of breath, for running at an elevation of fifty-six hundred feet, in an African sun, is not the easiest form of exercise.

Then we turned our repulsive beast over and disgustedly drew out the arrow heads, after which we retraced our course, found the antelope and after some manœuvring were able to dispatch him with another shot.

Next day we took it upon ourselves to kill two more hyenas. One of these Young shot at eighty yards while running. The arrow hit him in the neck, cut his jugular vein, and he lived but a few minutes.

This particular beast was greatly distended in the abdomen, so after skinning him, we opened the stomach and found that he had eaten an entire young Grant's gazelle: hide, bones, hoofs, head and all.

On our way home, much against our inclination, we collected a large male baboon for the Natural History Museum of Los Angeles, also a very rare specimen, a honey badger.

We had of course several long shots at Topi and Kongoni during the day, with our arrows, but these were blanks and taken mostly to see how close we could come, rather than with any hope of hitting. But when an arrow does strike at ranges up to two hundred yards, it loses none of its killing effect, so we had method in our madness.

We have camouflaged our bows by painting them an olive drab to harmonize with the prevailing colors of the landscape, and we are laying our plans for the real type of hunting for which our weapons are suited, that in which the object of the hunter is to outwit his quarry and capture him by woodcraft and nerve.

.   .   .   .

This letter is being sent out by native runners, who will travel some one hundred and sixty miles on foot. Then it will go by a creaking ox-cart to Nairobi, then by rail, then by ships lunging through the turbulent ocean, and finally at the end of two months it will land in your thriving little town of New York, halfway round the globe from our camp.

IV

A NIGHT IN THE BOMA

April 21st, 1925.

WE have at last undertaken the study of the lion problem. In the past we have killed mountain lions in California with the bow and arrow. We have slain grizzly bear in Wyoming and Alaska with our arrows. But the use of dogs and ambush made it possible there to obviate a direct attack by the beast. In Africa, neither of these defensive factors can be employed.

It is true that Paul Rainey and A. J. Kline, in taking pictures, have used dogs on lions, but in each instance these men have been backed up by professional hunters with heavy guns.

The use of a brush ambush, called a "boma," is quite the usual method of hunting lions by the less experienced big game hunters, especially in Kenya Colony. It is safe to say that nine out of ten lions are shot this way. Only the more expert hunters go out in the open themselves and withstand the charge of this infuriated beast.

A NIGHT IN THE BOMA

Of course with the bow, it is impossible to stop a charging lion, for death depends upon hemorrhage when an arrow is used, and this takes a few minutes at best, while the beast needs but a few seconds to complete his charge and do his murderous act.

If a gun is employed to assist an archer, we call it a complete failure from our standpoint. We never count animals in our bag that have been shot with bullets. All must be done clean by the strength of our good long bows and the keen flight of our arrows.

It is our hope to use spearmen to back us in our ultimate lion hunting, to act as a life insurance in place of gunpowder. So far, we have not negotiated with these people for this assistance, but shall do so on our next move to the volcanic district of Ngorongoro.

In the meantime we wanted to prove to our safari and to ourselves that we could kill these beasts with our bows.

Up to date we had seen some nine or ten lions and had even taken a shot or two at several, under what we considered safe conditions, but we knew that to make a complete demonstration, and still come off with enough man power left to carry out our expedition we must insure safety first. So we chose the boma.

Fortunately Simson had a boma in readiness for our use. He built it within a couple of miles of his camp, in a zone he had reserved for photography. Not only is Simson a mighter hunter before the Lord, like Nim-

31

rod of old, but he is a nature photographer. He does not spend all his time killing animals. In later years he has devoted most of his time to photographing them. Not only is he a photographer, but fortunately for us he is also an archer, and though he has not gone in for this sport particularly in hunting, he knows the difficulties that confront an archer, and has patience with this ancient method of getting game.

This particular boma he has used to obtain some of his best lion pictures, and no one has taken better. On one occasion he had twelve lions in a picture at once; six were feeding on a zebra bait. Upon another night, when he set himself the difficult task of collecting specimens of cubs for the Los Angeles Museum, he shot five small cubs with a 22-calibre rifle. Each animal he carefully shot through the lungs, and death was noiseless and immediate.

Unfortunately his sixth bullet went too high and broke the cub's back. The little one cried with pain and instantly the mother charged the boma. She tried to plunge through the aperture made for camera work and almost succeeded in gaining entrance when Simson shot her in the throat and killed her. This seemed to attract more lions and another female dashed at the opening, roaring with rage. He shot her, when such pandemonium broke out as few men have heard and survived.

At least a dozen beasts attacked the boma, raging

THIS IS A BOMA

at the brush closed exit and the window, running around and around, roaring so that the very chest walls of Simson and his gun bearer shook and vibrated with the thunderous tones. Dumbfounded by the fierceness of the attack, and seeking to avoid further provocation, Simson and his man Kazimoto crouched in a dark corner of the boma and rigidly refrained from flashing on the light till the hubbub subsided. It took nearly two hours for the beasts to leave.

Any man who proclaims that such an episode would not rouse fear in his soul, is deceiving himself, but no one else.

We used this very boma for our first real trial of the arrows.

Simson sent out an expedition to shoot a zebra and drag it about in a wide circuit, finally tying it securely to a tree some fifteen yards in front of the boma. I might say that this brush ambush is a corral some eight feet wide by twelve long, made by lashing poles to trees with bark strips, and covering the sides for a height of six or seven feet with palm leaves and thorn brush.

A small aperture in the rear permits entrance, and is stopped by a large bundle of thorn bush being pulled in to fill the hole. In front is a long open space between two parallel poles, the height of the chest. This permits seeing the bait and shooting arrows out.

The dead zebra was covered with thorn brush to

33

keep off hyenas and vultures and left over night. Next day we sent two natives to inspect and report progress. They reported that a lion had taken the bait, a leopard had entered the boma and that hyenas had cleaned up the fragments.

We repeated the performance, giving them another zebra so that they might get the free lunch habit. Zebra are natural lion food in this country, and apparently good for nothing else. They occur in tens of thousands about here and are classified as pests.

Next night the bait was taken again, so we decided to occupy the boma on the third evening.

After an early supper, we journeyed down to the boma before sunset, the four of us: three archers, Young, White and I, with Simson to handle the flash light.

Sitting in a jungle boma on an African night offers many features of interest. Of course we keep absolutely silent, do not smoke, show no light, and hardly move.

Night descends; the birds give their evening calls; the dove colored sky streaked with fading gold melts into dusky azure. The stars come out and the night sounds arise. The insects tune up for their long concert: the locust and the flying moth; the boring beetle in the dead limbs of the boma clicking out his death watch; the distant short bray of a zebra, resembling the bark of a small dog; the call of a night hawk; the wailing chatter of a hyena all fill the minor numbers of the evening program. Then in the distance we hear the rumble of a lion's roar.

Off in another quarter an answering grumbling bass note tells that the hunting game is on, and that soon the convergence of prowling predatory beasts will round up their quarry and the killing will begin.

A jackal gives his querulous little bark as he approaches the bait. Darkness has fallen and we sit in the gloom. Now the insane laughter of a hyena sounds close at hand, and pattering feet tell us the entrance of these detestable creatures on the scene. Suddenly there is a scurrying of padded feet and all is quiet.

A soft purring grunt denotes a lion's approach and all other animals leave in haste. Your heart goes at gallop speed and your breath is held from jerking by a conscious effort. A lapping sound comes clicking in the darkness, you can all but see great furry tongues licking in the pool of blood that rests in the disembowelled carcass outside the boma.

We wait and wait, then softly creep to the aperture. Our bows are ready strung, our quivers strapped upright to the framework of the enclosure. We nock our arrows and rise slowly, shafts drawn to the head.

On goes the brilliant white light and in startling distinctness there lies the striped hindquarters of the zebra, the dense thorn background, and three lions standing or crouching in the spotlight!

35

No one knew what a lion would do when struck with an arrow. There are no statistics on the point.

We shot together. We struck! Two beasts bounded out of vision and not a sound occurred. The third lion stood dazed in the glare of light. I drew another arrow quickly and shot.

Simson saw it hit her neck, then all was blank.

The flashlight went out and absolute black dropped before our eyes. Off in the night we heard the whining grunt of a lion, presumably wounded with an arrow. This slowly faded in the distance and the minor sounds of the night arose to audibility again.

We retired to the back of the boma with hardly a whispered word, to let our racing pulses settle down. For almost an hour we sat in the gloom, no small beasts came to the bait. We knew that lions still were about. The distant roar of a great old male came from the open veldt.

Then out of the immediate stillness, with never a preliminary note, we heard that licking, lapping sound. Lions were at the bait!

Again we flush with eagerness and turbulent mixed emotions. We creep to the boma window, nock our arrows, rise, and on goes the flash.

Two lions are in illumination. The larger, apparently a female, lies broadside to us, her head at the zebra's side. All three archers shoot at her. We hear the welcome thud of striking arrows, there is a

36

bounding streak of yellow light, a grunt of surprise and pain, and the stage is empty, save for the dead striped bait.

Out in the night we hear a lion cough. She coughs and breathes hard and tries to roar, but seems unable to force the air from her throat. A pang of sympathy strikes us. She is grievously wounded: lung shots!

Soon the sounds grow faint. Either she is dying or dragging herself off to the donga, thick in reeds and grass.

A distant roaring tells us that an old male is working in toward the boma. "Come on, old boy, come on!" we whisper. The snoring, coughing grunt comes nearer, and we wait with repressed breathing for the mighty fellow.

But here the climax drags. Our noble friend without is far too wise to come close. His courage is unimpeachable, but his caution is praiseworthy. He never came to us; but after long and ominous protest, his rumblings faded in the distance.

Hour followed hour. Some in the boma dozed while others watched. We felt confident that we had struck three lions, and that at least one lay dead near the boma.

Hyenas came to tear and crunch the carcass outside. Sometimes we frightened them away with the flash, sometimes we shot at the shifty beasts with our arrows. At last we let them feed, and dawn began to wake the birds.

Early in the gray light we sallied forth with great caution, and with chagrin each picked up one or more of his futile arrows. We had not struck as often as we thought. Still we all agreed that one lion at least must lie dead near about. A broken shaft and blood stains showed that we had hit.

We searched in vain. The donga, or shallow creek bed, was only a couple of hundred yards off and this jungle of thick cover, no sane man would enter, knowing that some six or eight lions lay hidden there, and two at least were wounded.

We scouted all over the plains and made all the racket and disturbance we could on the outskirts of the jungle, but no sound returned. So we set two boys to watch and returned to camp, considerably crestfallen and disappointed.

There is no satisfaction in wounding any animal and letting it escape, no matter how cruel and bloodthirsty that beast may be. We fully believed that one lion died and that at least one other was mortally wounded but we had no positive evidence.

At evening we returned to get the report of the boys and to see if the vultures told their whereabouts; but the jungle gave forth no sign.

Young and I sat out another night in the boma. Rain fell on us, hyenas and jackals howled and barked.

A NIGHT IN THE BOMA

Simba, the great lion, prowled and roared off in the distance; herds of zebra stampeded past the boma and soft purring grunts circled us not far off, but no lions came in the circle of light.

Weary with waiting and stiff with the cold and wet, we wandered back to camp for breakfast.

Our lion encounter to date is inconclusive and not to our liking. We must remember, however, that all shooting is cruel, though one can gloss over the facts of the sport.

If we forget that life itself is a cruel contest, especially in the wilds, then we are shocked and pained by the hunters' story. We should avoid details.

So far as the arrow is concerned it is no more painful than a bullet, only more visible.

The most distressing wounds are those of shattered bones. An arrow cannot do this but it produces death quickly when properly placed.

It is the fair contest, the sporting chance, the thrill of the chase and the conflict of emotion that give sanction to taking animal life.

If we cannot feel this, we should never go hunting, nor read tales of it.

V

THE FIRST LION

April 25th, 1925.

WE have killed our first lion with the bow and
arrow!

For the past week great herds of wildebeest
have been swarming into the country and their migra-
tory progression reminds one of the mighty multitude
of bison that roamed the prairies of America fifty
years ago.

The lions have followed these animals, making their
kills. Every night we have heard the unmelodious blat
of these awkward wildebeest, these gnu, with their large
solemn heads, their long straight manes, their white
beards, their bodies tapering abruptly to the tail, their
stiff-legged though swift gallop, these comedy cows.

Restless and ever on the move, they had invaded
our territory from some dry region, coming by tens of
thousands, and attended by a horde of grewsome
camp followers: lions, hyenas, jackals, and vultures.

It is a strange thing in this country of incessant murder, that there is not a carcass, a dried skin, not a hoof

nor a bone left bleaching on the veldt. One never sees the sad remains; they simply don't remain.

On some of our hunts here, where we have left the skinned body of a beast, we have returned in half an hour to find nothing there. A slinking hyena and a hundred stupid gorged vultures hang about and have a satisfied look, that's all!

So with the coming of the wildebeest the lions have greatly increased in number, and we have taken advantage of the time to add to our experience in the hunting of these dangerous cats. We have had frustrated encounters with a number up to date and are gathering knowledge of their ways.

To give some idea of the nature of these great cats, let me digress a moment to relate our experience in photographing two other lions. One of these was a fretful female. We approached her within a distance of forty yards, when just as we snapped the camera, and with no further provocation, she instantly charged and came at us with stifled grunts and long bounding leaps. In the wink of an eye she was upon us and was only crumpled and stopped at the deafening explosion of two heavy rifles. Her quivering body lay five paces from us, her intent to kill in every twitching muscle.

The second specimen was a beautiful black-maned lion, at whom we shot a few unsuccessful arrows, one or two of which wounded him slightly, as he crouched at bay. We wished to take a picture of him.

He was a surly old lord of the jungle and had recently been defeated in a family fight. No sooner did we get him in photographic range than he let out a roar that shook the heavens and charged our group. As he came on he lunged and pounded the ground like a race horse, each impact of his massive feet accompanied by a sonorous cough. White and Simson opened fire on him as he galloped toward us, but failed to bring him down.

Straight for Simson he leaped. Two guns fired again and the slug from Simson's second barrel struck him in the face as he rose in air before us. He was knocked end over end, turned a full somersault and landed ten feet beyond our party as we dodged his mighty fall.

That's close enough! That's how they come!

The range necessary for photography, from forty to eighty yards, is practically the same as that used in archery.

It must be remembered that no man has hunted lions with the bow and arrow since the days of the Assyrian kings several thousand years ago, so we did not know what the outcome of such an adventure would be.

Mind you, we never contemplated stepping out in the jungle and slaying the king of beasts with our archery tackle. We can't stop a charging lion, though we can kill one. Even the ancient royal hunters shot from chariots with their horses running in retreat from the lion's charge.

But a lion is only flesh and blood. He responds to physiologic reactions as do all other animals. His heart and lungs and great vessels are as easy to cut with a sharp broadheaded arrow as those of any other body. He will die as quickly from hemorrhage as a sheep or a deer. Now we have proved it, I will go on with the story.

Three or four days ago, time goes so noiselessly in Africa where excitement is the order of the day, we started bright and early for our quest of lions.

We struck the trail of the wildebeest and waded through them. They seemed nervous and unusually petulant from loss of sleep and the ceaseless harassment of their enemies.

In the early hours of the morning when the sky looks cool yet blushing and a grey veil seems to stretch across the veldt, one can often see the leisurely pacing of lions, slowly retiring to the shade of the deep grass after the night shift is done. Even in the early warm light of morning one can see them sunning themselves and resting from their midnight prowls.

So we journeyed over the open spaces and sought the elevated ridges, from which we searched the land with our glasses.

Our bows had been carefully overhauled, our arrows sharpened to the keenest possible edge. We carried about fifteen in each of our quivers. In case of accident we had our first aid surgical dressings, with plenty of permanganate in readiness. Lion wounds, if not immediately fatal, are almost invariably fatal from septic infection within a week. Permanganate is the best agent to combat this if applied immediately. We had plenty, and we had our *nerve* along. So we rattled across the open country in our little auto that looks like a butcher's delivery car.

We progressed leisurely and the sun rose to a pleasant warmth. About eight o'clock we sighted two female lions in the open, making their way back to cover. We set out at a rapid pace to intercept them. By Leslie's good tactics we succeeded in getting between the larger of these animals and the dense grass of the donga. One lioness made a hurried cut across our front and eluded us. The larger of the beasts hesitated at a hundred yards and looked us over.

The gaze of these animals is the most disdainful and insolent of any that I know. This lioness summed us up with a cool indifference that was astonishing. Never had her authority and supremacy been questioned, yet here were four bipeds who dared to edge between her and her accustomed haunts! It was our plan to follow her and as we got near the archers were supposed to jump out and run alongside the car ready to shoot. We carried out this method of attack.

At first she simply turned to one side as one with reserved impatience. We ran parallel to her course and again interposed ourselves between her and the

44

donga. With a look of indignant surprise she uttered a low threatening growl and switched her tail. We approached her closer.

She turned as if wishing to be rid of an obnoxious presence, yet not deeming it necessary to resort to physical violence. We were simply objectionable. On we went straight at her. Now she glared at us and planned her own battle. She picked out a group of wild fig trees and made a direct run for them.

With long swinging leaps she swept over the grass and quickly gained this shelter. There she stood at bay waiting for us.

Now something happened that very few Africanders have seen and which undoubtedly combined to favor our cause. The lioness seeing us still after her, leaped up into the low crotch of a tree, and stood there waiting for us. Lions never climb trees, but this lady was different.

She was undoubtedly influenced by our numbers and the car, and felt that her position was stronger from this location. As it proved later, she made a mistake. For, while her body was sheltered from our shafts by the limbs of the tree, the lioness was stationed in a poor attitude to charge. Simson brought the car to a sudden stop, and he and White got out with their rifles. Young and I were already on the ground.

We came up slowly but steadily to a distance of some forty yards, then Young and I opened fire with our bows.

45

Our first volley of arrows was shamefully wild and inaccurate, but they served to rouse her temper to the fighting point. She roared forth her challenge and lashed her tail in defiance. We shot again.

Two arrows struck her in the head. She was furious! For an instant I thought she would bound from the tree and hurl herself upon us, but before this intention could become crystallized into action we struck her in the throat and again in the thigh. She wheeled to bite this last wound and grind the arrow shaft in her teeth.

While turned thus a keen arrow was driven deeply in her chest. Her rage was tremendous, but the last of her roar had the ominous gurgle of an animal shot in the lungs. We wasted arrows in feverish haste to drive home our victory and of these flying messengers of death another struck her full and hard in the center of her body and disappeared to the feather.

Blood rushed from her mouth and nose, great heaving sighs convulsed her body and she turned in the tree as if to flee. Then she fell lengthwise in the wide crotch, caught almost head down, and died.

It seemed incredible that so powerful and fearsome a beast could have died so swiftly and so easily from a few little shafts of wood tipped with steel. Yet there she was, as dead as the Assyrian kings!

Simson and White stood at the side lines and cheered us on or jeered at our poor shots. Now they grinned

46

A DEAD LION IN A TREE

and said those things that are dear to the heart of the tyro. They knew that we had done a most unique thing, foolhardy, perhaps, yet we had proved it could be done as our ancestors in the chase had done before us.

In all, Young and I shot twenty-nine arrows at this lioness as she lunged back and forth behind the protecting limbs. Thirteen shafts were driven deep in the tree, seven were in her body and the rest flew off into the African landscape. It was admittedly poor shooting, but this was our first lion.

It is no easy thing to jump out of a bouncing car, run at a dizzy pace up to a lion at bay and then steady down to the technique necessary for accurate bow shooting. We drew near and looked at the dead beast.

There she lay, and in less time than it takes to tell it. Hardly three minutes elapsed between the first arrow and the time when she turned in the wild fig tree and fell head downward, lifeless, the strangest sight in Africa.

As for our emotions, I leave them to your imagination.

When we arrived in camp there was great excitement among the natives over our achievement. All the boys had to shake Young and me by the hand and express their glee and approbation. Later on in the day they decorated our hut with flowers and after retiring to the river they returned with their bodies daubed with white paint, wearing fantastic head dresses of grass and leaves, carrying wands and clubs; they came in mass formation chanting the lion song. They circled around us, went through grotesque gestures and mimic combat; they roared like Simba, then with a great stamping of their feet and wild shouts they hoisted us on their shoulders and paraded through the camp.

At last they wore themselves out and set us down. As they gathered in a circle about us, smiling and sweaty and happy at their own performance, we knew it was our turn to act. So we did the correct thing in Safari etiquette; we gave them a bright new shilling apiece.

And so the day ended.

VI

MORE LIONS

April 30th, 1925.

A RTHUR YOUNG and I are sitting in a blind
near the Sironera River, waiting for game, our
long sharp arrows and strong graceful bows by
our side. This morning we are photographing game,
and if chance presents a fair shot we will take it with
the bow. While we wait I write this note.

The past week has been a strenuous one for us and
for the lions. This completes our second week in
Tanganyika and we have seen over ninety different
lions. A game hog with his battery of rifles could
have killed fully a third of these noble beasts. We
have taken the pelts of twelve.

Of this number we have shot four with the bow and
arrow and eight with the gun. These latter were
lions that charged at close quarters after we attempted
to photograph them, or after having shot at them
with arrows.

In some instances the charges have been terrific and

49

the oncoming animal has been stopped at a few paces from our group. The gun on these occasions is a life saving institution, but from an archer's standpoint it is a confession of weakness, and as archers we hereby confess our utter incapacity to stop charging lions without tackle. The part the gun man plays in the game we look upon as a necessary evil so far as we are concerned. In itself, it is of course a fair sport, but one so often told in African tales that there is no great novelty in it. Any good game shot equipped with the requisite artillery can and does succeed at this lion business.

To be charged by a galloping, grunting, deadly lion, is exhilarating, especially when one has the feeling of security given by modern explosives and rifle perfection. You can stand as I do, and calmly snap the camera.

But that is not the saga we would sing. That is an oft told tale of the modern "mighty hunter." We would sing of the bow, the weapon that gave man his first triumph over his predatory enemies and crowned his brow with the laurels of victory in battle.

In the bow and flying shaft man hurls his own soul at the mark. It is part of him, and when he strikes, he has fairly won his game. He calls on no magic from the clouds, no favors from the gods.

But the bow has its limitations, otherwise modern ingenuity would not have sought mightier weapons.

The limitations of the bow can be supplemented and greatly advanced by the use of allied primitive arms. We speak of the shield and the spear. These are comrades in arms. These are the very things we want in our archaic pursuit of dangerous game.

On these very plains where we today are assaulting lions, two years ago A. J. Kline brought a small band of African natives, the Nandi. Ten of these men attacked and killed three charging lions with their spears. Absolutely nude except for their gorgeous headdress, armed with spears, throwing knives and buffalo hide shields, they challenged and overcame one lion after another with utmost bravery. Kline took moving pictures of them as they received the infuriated attack on their shields and annihilated the oncoming beast with their spears. That is real sport, compared with which the white man's gun game is pitiable.

We could do this too, if we had the numbers and the requisite practice, for the white man can do what any man can do, and usually does it better. Gladly would we risk injury for the thrill of such a triumph. With the bow to hurl defiance and skilfully strike at a distance, then with the spear to meet the charge if needed, our sport would indeed be a royal one, fit for men and lions.

In all the ancient battles the archer was a deadly auxiliary of the army, but he always needed protection from charging cavalry. For this defense, spear-men, trenches, shields and spikes were used. 'Twas ever thus! But the arrows won most battles in medi-æval times. The arrow is adequate to slay the king of beasts, this we know now from our own experience. More than this, where the shaft can be placed in a lion, it distracts his attention from the hunter to the arrow. He fights this and thus permits another shot and it delays the charge till death overtakes him.

I have an undeveloped film there in my knapsack, of a great lion rearing, rampant, and striking vainly with his heavy muscled arm, at my white arrow in his forehead. In that very attitude my companion, Arthur Young, drove another arrow in his heart and killed him.

This lion is our last, slain with bow, last of four. He was brought to bay in the long grass of the veldt, and lay lashing his tail and muttering threats, some sixty-five yards off.

This is good shooting range for our bows. The heavy hunting arrows travel nearly "point blank" at this distance. So we started in on him. After a flight or two we had his distance and began hitting him. Our shooting had improved. As he was struck by one arrow, then another, he lunged at the offending shaft and ground it in his teeth, he even bounded out a short way to seize those that fell short and destroy them. Later, when he was dead we found the feathered ends of two in his throat where he had tried to swallow them.

This particular animal not only was struck in the head and heart, but a deep penetrating wound through the liver and blood vessels of the abdomen flooded his body with blood and would also have been fatal.

He died an archer's trophy, nearly four hundred pounds in weight and nine feet in length.

As a surgeon I perform the autopsy on all these beasts that we slay, not only to ascertain the exact nature of their wounds and the destructive nature of our missiles, but to learn what diseases these creatures of the open space have. I have been requested moreover, by Dr. Mentzner of the Mayo Clinic, to make a study of the comparative anatomy of the gall ducts of all the African species of mammalia that fall within our observation. This I am doing. The knowledge thus gained is directly applicable to the problem of gall bladder surgery in the human.

Sensitive souls who cannot bear to hear of blood or interior anatomy should avoid reading these field notes, for we are in a land of stalking death and grewsome realities.

The two other lions killed with our bows were shot at distances of sixty-eight yards and forty-six yards, respectively. Both were large males. The first received an arrow wound deep through the chest and diaphragm, the second was transfixed by a feathered

53

shaft through the abdomen, besides minor injuries. In this case the beast refused to charge and the wounds would have been eventually fatal, but to bring his suffering to an end, Young shot him with a gun.

One of these brutes feigned a charge and White shot at him with a rifle. The bullet only grazed the skin of the abdomen, and the lion died later from its arrow wounds. This we refused to count as our trophy because it was touched by a bullet.

The hide of a lion is extremely tough and often an arrow goes diagonally through the body and bulges the hide on the opposite side. We have shot completely through a full-sized lion, side on, and had the arrow carry several yards past him.

In the instance of the lion shot in the heart, this arrow entered at the shoulder, pierced the heavy muscles of this region without striking bone, and penetrated the chest wall by cutting the second rib in two.

We have seen bullets from a 405 Winchester and a Springfield rifle stopped by no greater resistance, and lodge harmlessly in the flesh. The real stopping of lions charging from short distances was done by Leslie Simson's big double gun, 577 in calibre, delivered in brain crushing shots.

Our trophies are of course skinned in the field and will be brought back to America with us. During this skinning process we are subject to several annoyances,

SHE WANTED TO RIDE IN OUR CHARIOT

not the least of which is the attack made upon us by the swarm of lion flies that beset us. They seem to be a mixture between a fly, a tick and a bee and have a yellow fuzzy likeness and the pertinacity of a miniature lion. They cling and bite with ferocity, and even after one catches them in the hand they are tough and difficult to destroy. Then when you have the lion's hide safely in your possession, a migration of black ticks starts from the cooling skin of their late host, to the new and inviting fields of the hunter. They cause a distressing febrile reaction, that one would gladly avoid if possible.

Lions themselves seem quite subject to disease. They show evidence of old pneumonia; they have the mange and most of them entertain several kinds of intestinal worms. They have, moreover, in many instances, old and recently incurred wounds, in various stages of infection. These have been received in the family fights, which seem to mar their otherwise beautiful family life. They are also said to be quite if not completely monogamous; but sad to relate, when a female is bereft of her lord and master, through the evil intervention of some invidious hunter, the lonely lioness finds consolation and another mate almost the next night.

Having written this much I glance up as I've done many times during the scribble, and see the dusty herds of wildebeest hovering in the offing. They came

to drink twice, they and a herd of zebra together.
But the wind is strong and gusty and carries our scent
off on the plains, and they fear to come again. Up
wind from us a hundred Thomson's gazelles congre-
gated, fought among themselves and frolicked. Drinking they do but little. But the sequence of animals
seems to be quite a ceremony and they must come in
their proper order or not at all.

We arrived at the blind at daybreak, after being kept
awake a good part of the night by trampling droves of
zebras, belligerent lions within stone throw of our
huts and the devilish wails of hyenas.

The first comers to our watering hole were jackals,
pretty little creatures, more like our foxes than a coy-
ote. They are graceful and intelligent. Yesterday
we saw one off on the veldt walk up to a gluttonous
hyena, bluff him into dropping a hunk of meat and
run away with it, while an envious vulture flopped
his funereal wings nearby and laughed, silently.

After the jackals at the pool, come birds: parra-
keets, sand grouse, doves and small fry. Then come
the dainty Tommies, then zebra and wildebeest, all
dashing into the water and making it muddy, starting
at the clatter of a pebble and all rushing out again.
Then they wheel and slowly approach, some leader
braying and calling assurance to the rest. We snap a
camera and off they rush. After an hour slowly the
Topi, those large lugubrious antelope, come in small

56

numbers and draw near to drink. Here they come now, and Young fixes his camera for another shot while I crouch low in the boma and finish these last few words of the epistle.

VII

THE RHINO AND TEMBONI

May 2nd, 1925.

WE have just returned from our first rhino hunt with the bow. Two days ago we left for a spot some twenty-five miles south, in the direction of the volcano Lemargrut. Here are level plains for thirty or fifty miles in extent. Strange to say there is no great abundance of game here, but giraffe, ostrich and rhinoceros occur in fair numbers. This part of Africa is not particularly well supplied with animals.

Arrived at our destination we camped near a fine large cave in the rocks of a kopje. This cavern had served as a refuge for hunters before: they were Wandorobo, or wild men, who devote their entire time to hunting. In the cave we found a great quantity of animal bones and picture paintings on the wall, done in clay, charcoal and wax.

These men hunt with poisoned arrows and by driving game into pits. They are not popular with the other natives nor with the whites, because of their nomadic life and their destruction of game.

The outlook from the Wandorobo cave is over a beautiful grassy plateau, broken at intervals by rocky outcroppings on which thick vegetation has grown. These kopjes are favorite sites for rhino to browse, and also for baboons and leopards to inhabit.

In preparation for the rhino, we have made especially heavy and long pointed arrows. The heads are seven inches long, an inch and a half wide, and as thin as a knife blade. They are very carefully tempered and sharpened. We consider that it is the friction on the shaft that stops an arrow's penetration, and a long head reaches in to a vital area better than a short. The shafts of this missile are particularly rigid wood, and the feathers come from the greater bustard, or pau. These are the finest and most closely knit feathers we have ever seen, entirely suited to steer so massive an arrow head.

These heads are as sharp as daggers and we greased them in lion fat to expedite their penetration.

We also carried our heavy bows. Ordinarily I shoot with a seventy or seventy-five pound yew bow. This time I took an eighty-four pound lemonwood bow heavily backed with rawhide, while Young took along his heavy Osage bow, requiring ninety pounds' pull on the string to draw a 28-inch arrow to the head.

On the afternoon of our arrival, while White was

59

reciting a bit of comic doggerel about a rhino, suddenly our coveted beast barged into sight. He had come around the kopje and winded our outfit so when first seen he was under full sail and tacking off in a general southeasterly direction at twelve knots an hour.

Neither Young nor I had ever seen a wild rhino before. We had tossed peanuts at them in a circus, but this business of meeting one in the "great open spaces" is quite different. Young said: "Well, he certainly is some hunk of meat!"

As conditions were, and from the general state of his nerves, apparently it was advisable to finish our luncheon and locate our pachydermatous friend after he had regained his equanimity. So we went on lunching, and Mr. Rhino at last came to anchor in the shade of a sheltering thorn tree off on the veldt.

He stood there in oafish thought for an hour or so, then shifted his position further out on the prairie, near to nothing at all, with his head down wind so he could see everything he could not smell. He was in no position to be approached, still we started out to stalk him in hope that something would turn up to favor our cause.

We stole down a shallow donga and got behind the tree beneath which he once stood. He was about 250 yards off. We crept through the long grass trying to circle to a nearer tree, and were progressing nicely when up on the rocks of the kopje some baboons began to chatter and squawk and then a Korhaan bird flew overhead and gave its warning cry. Then slowly we could see primordial thought sweep over the brain of this antediluvian monster. It seemed to take hours to sink into his soul or that place where his brain ought to be. We could see him adding up his experiences thus: "I smelled a man." "I heard a scared baboon." "The Korhaan bird gave warning." "Q. E. D. It is time to leave"—and he did. He set his compass due south and put on full steam ahead. When last seen he was pointed in the general direction of Johannesburg and looked about the size of a black shoe button on the horizon.

We straightened out our backs and returned to camp. "We will meet you later on Gunga Din!"

So we slept last night on the thick green grass of the veldt and left just as the sun rose this morning. We scouted the country for our recalcitrant friend, but a most unusual fog drifted over the land, possibly arising off Lake Eyassi some sixty miles away. So we gave up the search temporarily and set out for our base camp.

On the way home we chanced to see a lone bull eland standing in a meditative mood beneath a tree, at noon. By good fortune we were able to approach him within bow shot, and got an arrow into his flank. He galloped off, but he could not run fast because of his chest wound, so we overtook him and by following him up in his disabled condition, struck him again with our arrows and ultimately finished him with a couple of shafts deep in the chest.

This largest member of the antelope family is a magnificent beast, weighing in some instances two thousand pounds. His proportions are graceful; his horns are like well turned corkscrews; he has a slight hump and a moderate dewlap; a fine grained hide and most delectable meat. I believe that the eland is easily domesticated and as such he would be a splendid addition to our stock ranges.

We also shot another Tommy at some forty yards and secured him in a most expeditious manner; he travelled hardly a hundred yards after being hit with an arrow.

I think there are few better meats in the world than those of eland and Tommy.

The fact that we do not use poison on our arrows seems to worry our native friends. The Wakamba and the Wassukuma, who constitute the majority of our porters are both aboriginal bowmen and always use poison. They obtain this by boiling pieces of wood from a certain tree they call Kibyi and reducing the extract to a black residue like tar. This they smear on a fore shaft or shank which becomes detached after the barbed head strikes the animal. They say that such a victim travels less than two hundred yards before dropping dead.

AN ELAND

THE RHINO AND TEMBONI

The Sultani of Ikoma having heard that we were
shooting lions with the bow, sent over a present of a
bow and a quiver of arrows. I shall test the poison
for its physiologic properties when we return to America. We sent the Sultani a fifty cent bracelet and a
Boy Scout pocket knife and he has been overcome with
the munificence of our gifts. In his prostrated condition, however, he did not lose his presence of mind,
but has made a request for meat. Probably a lowly
zebra will fill the bill.

Besides the friendly interchange of royal greetings, a
straggling band of native archers has fallen upon us
armed to the teeth and dressed in an innocent smile.
They have come to see the strange white men who shoot
the bow and arrow and to compete with them in their
national sport.

The first of these redoubtable archers was one Temboni which means: "Near the Elephant." He is a wily
old villain and a poacher in every fibre of his skinny
body. He brought two bows and a quiver of poisoned
arrows. He brought also a present of yams for Leslie
Simson. A toto, or small native boy, was attached as
camp follower; he carried the luggage.

This big-eyed little coon had a red fez cap as his one
article of adornment, and after his thirty-five mile hike
from Ikoma he was as fresh as any street urchin usually is. Temboni challenged us to shoot against him.
First he inspected our long yew bows very carefully

and tested the edge of our broadhead arrows. His own bows were good and strong, pulling possibly seventy pounds, but quite stubborn and inelastic at the last of the draw. We have a straw target at forty yards and a bit of cardboard six inches square pinned on this.

We shot at this piece of paper and registered a hit every second or third shot. He could hardly hit the three-foot straw mat. The distance is more than he is accustomed to. He shoots from blinds at ten and twenty yards.

We then shot for distance. His best shafts flew something short of two hundred yards. My light trim arrows reached a distance of nearly two hundred and seventy-five yards.

He was overcome with admiration and amazement, protesting that our arrows were like bullets.

So after an exchange of professional compliments the "shauri," as they call all social, political or military events in this land, was ended. Both parties withdrew to their respective camps in perfect order without the loss of a single archer.

VIII

WATCHING IN A BLIND

May 9th, 1925.

THE rainy season has set in and heavy thunder clouds gather in the sky as I write. Nearly every afternoon we have rain, either several gentle showers or a blinding deluge of water falling as a cataract from Heaven.

So we have had to abate our hunting somewhat. The mornings generally are clear and bright, but the ground is too soft for extensive travel.

The new moon held her horns up and promised a dry month; the natives looked at this and said: "No rain." But the zebra left the country and the female "Tommies" began dropping their young, anticipating green grass, and the flies clustered in the bandas, or open palm huts, and the rains came.

It is what the animals know and do that is most interesting. Watching as we have from bomas, we have observed things that probably one can read in many African game books; still our own discoveries always seem most important to ourselves.

Our last boma was built in a large thorn tree, near a water hole, and resembled a great nest, some fifteen feet off the ground, reached by a rustic ladder in the back. All evidence of building had been carefully removed, and the animals seemed to pay no attention to it.

It is an annoying fact that animals when they come to water, always come up wind, so they can detect danger. We hoped that an elevation would help to carry our scent over their heads and permit us to maintain our position of advantage. White occupied this particular boma and relates that the first morning a wild goose came to water and having drunk came out on the bank, cast an inquisitive eye up at the strange large nest, and flopped up to its edge where it sat turning its head from side to side looking at the nest and its occupants. Then it gravely stepped inside and sat among them. White reached out a hand to catch its leg, when off it fluttered, a very greatly surprised goose.

At night, only the predatory animals come to drink. You hear the gentle lapping of jackals, and then the noisy gulping of hyenas. Lions drink, but we have not heard them. Then there is a space in the early dawn when no beasts come. Soon after sunrise, the birds appear. Among the first are the sand grouse. They arrive in flocks, flying like pigeons and uttering a squawking crackle as they fly. They settle on the

66

ground in rows, in the order of their coming: one row behind the other. There may be hundreds on the ground at once waiting to drink.

But drinking in Africa is always a ceremony, even among the animals. So they wait till the first row has rested and scratched and rustled in the dust, then advances to drink, after which the second row comes forward. So it progresses, one flock at a time. If by chance a group of birds becomes frightened and flies off before it has drunk, then it circles in the air and takes its position in the rear of the procession. As each band rises, it starts its travel song and wings rapidly off into space.

When a vulture comes to water, it limps and humps itself forward to the edge of the pool then gobbles and clucks the water into its ugly mouth and throat, then it raises its crooked neck and chokes it down.

A Kavirondo crane is a beautiful bird, stately and circumspect. He walked in quite a way from the veldt and approached the pool with dignity and caution. Our nest did not escape his eye. The slightest movement on our part, even though we thought ourselves shielded by leaves, was detected by the crane. But this did not frighten him. When assured that we were no enemy to birds he continued his stately walk to the pool, drooped his crested head and by a quick thrust, scooped a bill full of water at one movement and swallowed it like a gentleman.

A few dips satisfied him and he went on his way, looking at the world about him with a kindly deliberate eye, and attending strictly to his own business.

After the birds, antelope come to drink.

The most graceful of these is the Thomson's gazelle. He is the cleanest little fellow! He has no flies or ticks upon him. His coat is always spotless and he is perfect in his manners.

Out on the plains where we have shot at him, one of these little chaps will feel himself at a safe distance from which to observe the new creature, man, and then when we shoot he will dodge the oncoming arrow.

It is not that an arrow shot from our eighty-pound bows has a slow, cumbersome flight; it is swift. But the Tommy is swifter. Even when preoccupied, such as scratching his ear with his hind hoof, your arrow probably will be seen and dodged before it strikes. Our American animals, except possibly the rabbit, are not such keen dodgers as these Africanders. All of these herbivora seem to be quick on the jump. An old Topi, an antelope the size of an elk, will apparently be viewing the landscape, sleepily, when an arrow starts for him, or if he sees you in surprise he starts off at a lunge, swerves to the left and then to the right so quickly that his body almost lays at a 45-degree angle, then gallops off. While a wildebeest does the same thing, he adds to his repertoire a kick with both hind feet, one to the left, one to the right; then a vicious hook with his horns and a great tossing of his funny head and mane, as if to show you how he would treat lions and all other troublesome creatures that worry a noble wildebeest.

Topi have a great habit of standing on ant hills and looking round the country. There is one old bull that has stood off on the plains opposite our camp and mounted guard on an ant hill when all other Topi have left the country. For years, Simson says, that same old bull has stood at that spot, with short intervals during the day for food and diversion, and seems to challenge all comers.

So far, though bands of Topi pass his way, I've never seen him have to fight for his ant hill, nor has he ever joined the gang. I presume he is a misanthrope with a perpetual challenge, a champion of a forgotten cause!

These animals don't seem to be afraid of lions in the daylight, and permit one to come quite close, when herded together.

On the other hand, the lion seems to be ashamed of his night calling and has an apologetic, sheepish air. Simson said he saw one full of meat being followed by a herd of hartebeest, and he slunk off with an occasional shamefaced turning of his head and dragging his tail, as if his one wish were to reach cover and avoid publicity.

During the past week, because of the rain, our hunt-

ing has been restricted; incidentally I have been laid
up in bed with a fever, probably acquired by sleeping
in bomas, down by the river where the sweet anopheles
dwell. I opine that it is not the proper thing to go to
the Tropics and not get fever.

Arthur Young, however, shot a good specimen of
wildebeest with the bow. He made a body shot at
fifty yards from a blind, and the beast ran off. Apparently, it had no knowledge of the nature of the insult
offered it, for it promptly ran back again to the same
position and Young shot a second arrow. This struck
it in the chest and dropped it dead. This last arrow
went completely through the animal at 45 yards and
stuck so hard in the ground that Young left it there to
show me.

But nothing escapes the eye of a Wandorobo hunter.
One of these strange creatures of the forest must have
seen his fellow archer make the shot, for soon a naked,
handsome, straight-nosed savage brought the arrow to
camp, all washed of blood. We thanked him and he
vanished.

Yesterday being my first day back on the firing line,
we thought we would take it easy, so we went out after
lions.

We found two full grown youngsters and separated
them by running between them with the car. One
instantly charged, even before our brigade was organized. There was a hasty call to arms, and our testy

friend was slapped severely in the face and chest, with the only effective argument for beasts of this sort;— high explosives. He discontinued his attack at a distance of three generous paces from our chariot.

Whether profiting by his brother's example, or because one member of the family had all the courage and the other all the good looks, I don't know, but the second lion proved a better general in retreat than in attack. We ran him to a standstill out on the veldt. There we got an arrow into him early, at seventy yards, and just as the prick of a hypodermic needle often makes an arrant coward of a man that ordinarily is most courageous even when stabbed or shot or beaten up by some friendly thug, so this beast lost his nerve completely. We shot at him repeatedly, missed him or hit him in areas not vital. He tried to bluff us off, but was not lion enough to come in. He turned and took another cover in the grass, growling and lashing his tail. This was his undoing. We reached him with our arrows, and after we had exhausted our quivers in long range shooting and running shots, we even went back to past locations, picked up our arrows and attacked him again. At last Young landed two good hits, one that cut his femoral artery in the thigh. Here we let him rest for more than half an hour, then as he lay exhausted with hemorrhage, Young drove a second shaft into his chest cavity and finished him off. Just as he died, however, we approached a little too near,

71

when, in one final burst of fury, he turned and threw himself several yards toward us. We jumped back to avoid a charge, and he sank to sleep weakened by a dozen arrow wounds.

He measured 39 inches at the shoulder, 72 inches body length, 30 inches tail; a total length of 8 feet 6 inches. His weight, as estimated by Simson who has weighed many lions, was well over 350 pounds. The skin of such an animal will measure 11 feet.

From this experience we have decided to establish a system of sticking up a little white flag at every stand from which we deliver a flight of arrows, so that we can mark our ground and thus return and find our ammunition when the show is over.

Because this particular beast preferred to run rather than fight, we wasted many arrows shooting at him while both parties were in motion, so we emptied our quivers ineffectively at him. We even called him the "cowardly lion," though I don't think he was. He was simply confused by the unusual circumstances of the situation. His Fabian tactics were his undoing.

· · · · · · ·

We present his picture, and you see he is after all a noble looking animal, now immortalized by this adventure.

THE COWARDLY LION

IX

NATIVE LIFE

May 13th, 1925.

THE natives in the vicinity of the camp are called Wassukuma. They are a fairly representative people of the country, not the best type, but peaceable, long suffering sort of human beings that make good porters and die by droves when the white man crushes them with the heel of civilization, as occurred in the late war. In ancient days they furnished the gangs of slaves that the Portuguese led out of the country with chains on their necks. They are hunters with the bow, and only incidentally agricultural and pastoral in their pursuits.

During the late war, Tanganyika was the theatre of diminutive military campaigns, and the Wassukuma were requisitioned as porters by both sides. The care given them was so bad, it is said, that hundreds died of overwork, starvation and disease.

It was quite natural then that they abandoned their villages and all took to the nomadic life in the bush,

73

which is so close to their native habit. Consequently, they raised no corn and could pay no annual hut tax. Now, hunting has been forbidden them with the object of forcing them to plant and raise crops. Each native must pay the British Government five shillings annually as a hut tax, and more if he has more than one wife. As it stands at present the Wassukuma have no chance to earn the five shillings except from occasional porter service or from the sale of wildebeest tails to other tribes. These of course they get by hunting.

Wildebeest tails are used as fly swatters by natives, also as decorative features to their costumes. So they are in steady demand, selling for a shilling apiece to the neighboring tribes.

Working as porters, as they do for Leslie Simson, and for other hunting safaris, these people earn about ten shillings a month, or two and a half dollars. Wages have gone up in modern days. A gun bearer earns sixty to eighty shillings a month. He must be an especially trained man, and risks his life for twenty dollars. But few can reach such heights as these.

Most Africans carry their loads on their heads but the Wassukuma carry their burdens on their shoulders and ordinarily pack sixty pounds all day long, usually fifteen to twenty miles.

We have just sent out thirty porters for gasolene and they are to be given a bonus of one shilling to each man that carries a case of petrol, or eighty pounds.

74

They were eager for the job and are due tomorrow from a two hundred and sixty mile jaunt.

Ten days ago they started out, each man with a stick and a rope, a little cotton blanket, a gourd of water and a bag of corn meal with dried meat. They carry no arms save a spear or two and a couple of bows and arrows that appear rather impotent when you remember that every night hyenas, leopards and lions circulate about their camp, and their watch fires are never overstocked with wood.

But they start out singing and come home on a trot, burdened heavily, but laughing and shouting. It's a wonderful disposition!

We get pumpkins and yams from Ikoma. There is also an old orchard there of limes and lemons planted by their oppressors, the Portuguese, three hundred years ago. We get this fruit from old M'Tone, the Sultani. This obsolete potentate stays in his metropolis, attended by his four wives, and well saturated in native beer. His reign is not very popular with the younger order of Wassukuma, but he hangs on till something else turns up. M'Tone sends us words of greeting and gourds of sour milk which we don't care to drink, even if it does prolong life. We send him safety pins and beads in return.

M'Tone's son, Masheki, the crown prince, is in camp with us; a very suave, intelligent fellow whose ambition in life seems to be to become a chauffeur. He watches every move of our native driver Kaki and is deeply interested in pumping up tires, tightening clutch bands and other intricate operations on the Ford truck. Masheki wears an old green plush hat and blue spiral puttees as his chief articles of raiment, showing a marked taste "pour la sporte."

Chickens we buy from Ikoma, at two and a half cents apiece. Eggs are just one-tenth of this, whatever that may be.

Here of course the shilling is divided into one hundred cents, a coin with a hole in the center like the Chinese cash, so one can carry them on a string. By this standard, chickens are ten cents each and eggs are one cent.

We carry a gunny-sack full of this coinage to defray our immediate expenses and buy potio. We hire twenty men and feed them for the price of one good servant in America.

Potio is their native corn meal, a red, coarse flour, that they boil up in earthen or tin pots and stir with a wooden paddle.

As a great treat, once in a while they are given salt. There is plenty of zebra meat in camp; they cut off great fat chunks of this and put them on sticks before the fire. We don't like zebra, but this yellow fatty meat is popular with the Wassukuma. It tastes like a combination between rancid butter and India rubber.

Our special boys, such as the tent boys and gun

COOKING POTIO

bearers, of course get better food: rice, tea, some sugar, salt and occasional leavings from our table. However, simple potio and meat is all they ask. They eat twice a day and drink the dirty water of the water holes without boiling.

The expeditionary force of native archers that we sent to Ikoma to get, and with which we expect to go on hunting trips, has not yet arrived. It is due this evening.

In the interim we have let up a bit on our strenuous hunting and during the past three days, since my last epistle, we have shot only one Tommy, a wildebeest and one lion. The wildebeest was shot by White with an arrow in the shoulder, too high to be immediately fatal. It ran off on the plains and eluded us. Evening came on and next morning we found its horns,—all that the lions had left.

The Tommy has disappeared into the stew kettle and the lion skin hangs out on the clothes-line in the back yard, or veldt.

This last trophy was not much in size. He was a half grown lion that we met out on the great open spaces, where cats are lions, and separated him from his family, especially his too solicitous mother.

He sought seclusion and safety in the tall grass of a donga. We tried to stone him out, then attempted to reconnoitre at close quarters. I was about to go around a certain thorn bush, but a nasty little limb

77

obstructed my path. I turned to retrace my steps when out pealed the most lusty roar that one could want to hear. Simson was at my back, and after we retreated in good order, though with some haste, he said, "Why, there must be another old female in there!" We worked around till we could see the swaying grass tops, then the glint of yellow hair and a lashing tail. I shot an arrow at the indistinct outline and heard it strike. With a grunt, out jumped our half grown lion, he with the mighty voice. He bounded off into another thicket. The arrow seemed to have punctured his enthusiasm to charge. So we followed him up, and again we let him have an arrow or two in the deep shadows of his retreat.

Out he leaped again and sought his first stand. We followed, and hit some more. After several of these shoot and jump episodes, we found blood in his tracks and he became more silent. At last we espied him lurking at the base of a tree, where we drove two arrows through his chest and pinioned him to the tree.

After a safe interval we approached and found him dead. We had to dig the arrow heads out of the wood with our knives to release his body. He was the size of a California mountain lion, six feet from tip to tip, weighing about one hundred and fifty pounds. But he had all the instincts of the African king of beasts, and was ready and anxious to charge. That first arrow, however, if it reaches home and this one seemed to

78

have struck him in the chest, that first arrow dampens ardor. The only trouble seems to be to get that arrow to connect up with the lion.

This makes the fifth lion to the credit of the bow.

Driving home after this episode, we were bumping along over the prairie when one of the party called out a warning. Simson turned the steering wheel just in time to avoid running over a tiny little gazelle curled up in the grass. We stopped the car and all alighted. There was a new born Granti no larger than a rabbit "playing possum" to avoid detection. His mother was several hundred yards away, feeding with a small herd.

We came close and stood over the little fellow, but he did not wink an eye and hardly breathed. We touched him gently and spoke softly to our little brother of the veldt. 'Tis said that nature protects these new born of the animal kingdom from predatory beasts by creating them devoid of body scent. To test this theory, I knelt down and placed my face close to his little form. There was no odor that a human might detect. But he smelled me and like a watch spring he uncoiled and leaped into my arms, thrusting his head in my open shirt front. I held him an instant then placed him on the ground, where he gathered his miniature legs under him, legs no larger than lead pencils, and galloped off over the plains, in puerile "buck jumps" and gay cavorting, the most spritely little beastie that ever came out of fairyland.

It was his first big adventure in life and he was so cocked up over it, the little rascal less than a foot high, he was a sight good for sore eyes!

Our blessing went with him and his mother did the rest.

X

A MIXED BAG

May 18th, 1925.

LIFE in our camp begins stirring about 4.30 A.M. The cook pokes the embers of the fire that burns near his little palm leaf shelter; the water boy begins rattling the petrol tins in which he heats water for the morning ablutions, and the tent boys crawl out of their hut and get ready to set the table and wake their Bwana.

Soon Hassan or Martini comes in our banda with a lantern and says: "Jambo Bwana"—"Good morning, Master," and we turn over beneath our mosquito nets and prepare to rise and dress. Hassan gathers everything in readiness and sees that we have it at hand. He would dress us if we would give him a chance, but Americans hardly enjoy this valet service as much as do our English cousins.

Soon we are at the breakfast table by lamp light, and have porridge, coffee, eggs and rye bread. The eggs we get from the industrious little native hens that run about the camp, eating lion flies off the hides as

81

they are fleshed, or picking at scraps of meat that lie around the skinning hut, and seeds from the wild grasses.

Our tent boys then gather our bows and quivers of arrows, bags of first aid dressings, canteens and cameras and place them all in the little Ford truck.

By this time the eastern sky is rosy and light, and the sun will come over the edge of the veldt promptly at six o'clock. It never varies more than a few minutes the year round, here beneath the equator. We start out at the earliest streak of dawn.

You must remember that we are a mixed party. Leslie Simson is collecting specimens for the Los Angeles Museum. He also acts as our life insurance agent with the heavy artillery, so he has a 22-calibre rifle and his heavy elephant gun on the front seat with him very handy. He steers the machine. Stewart Edward White seated in front is a liaison officer between the archers and the modern destroyer, so he carries a bow, a camera and a Springfield rifle. Arthur Young and I seated in the open box seat are the archers company and our equipment decorates the car in a gay fashion: powerful long bows and four or more quivers full of brightly painted arrows, usually fifty or sixty in number. Off we start over the veldt, to see what we shall see.

It is an amusing thing, that no matter how many countless head of game we pass, such as gazelles, wildebeest, zebra and kongoni, Simson will say, "Well, pretty soon we ought to see something!"—What he means by "something" is of course, lions. Usually we jog along till we do see them, and when we are done with them we pay attention to other game. We get our specimens, sometimes with the bow, if they are approachable, or with the 22 rifle. Game as large as Grant's gazelles Simson shoots with this small gun; and a varied bag we bring back at noon. Yesterday, for instance, we brought in a leopard, a fox, three mongoose, a marabout stork, a Tommy and a lion, and later in the afternoon we went out and got a specimen of female ostrich.

We were looking for lion, of course, and up at the edge of a distant hill we sighted two beautiful males coming home from a midnight forage. We raced to head them off from the wooded hill, and seeing us, they trotted across our front less than fifty yards off, neck and neck, like two clear cut figures on a medallion.

They made a beautiful sight. I jumped out to get a shot with the bow, and missed, much to my chagrin. They galloped rapidly over the crest of the hill and disappeared into a thorn thicket, out of which we failed to rout them.

While we were wandering around vainly looking for our lions, one of us espied a leopard skulking in the brush. It was a long distance off, with no hope of reaching it with the bow, and the wily beast had already seen us; so Art took a crack at it with Leslie's Spring-field rifle and made a center hit. Off loped the beast into the nearest jungle of thorns and aloes. We followed at a run and surrounded the thicket, throwing stones in its densest portions.

Soon we heard a low growl and knew the approximate location of our animal. We concentrated our rock barrage on this spot. How humiliating it is when a man grown you discover how awkward and weak you are at throwing stones! As a boy you could hurl a rock in a bush of this sort with precision and force; now you find you throw like a woman and only toss it in the general direction of the object.

The leopard failed to respond to the shower of missiles, so at last we decided to go in, to see if he were dead, though we didn't think so.

I was stationed outside and instructed to observe if he escaped on my side, incidentally to get behind a good sized tree, in case any artillery fire were necessary, from the jungle.

The others took a large brush knife or panga and began making their way into this mass of inhospitable vegetation. One man cut his way, while two others guarded him with their rifles. I heard them advancing, and as I stood looking for an outbounding leopard, two beautiful bright yellow bats flew from the cover, flopped noiselessly about for a moment in a dazzled state, then fluttered into another dark retreat.

After ten minutes I heard those inside saying that they had reached the blood-stained resting place of their quarry, but he had vanished.

We gathered our forces and trailed his spoor to another clump of thorns and sisal plants. Just as we approached the path by which he entered this, he came at us with a roar like a lion, a fierce and swift attack. The rifles banged as one, and the leopard was arrested in his spring and lay a defeated and vengeful beast, twenty feet from us. These animals, when wounded, are most determined in their charge, and for their size are more to be feared than a lion.

We robbed him of his skin and I presume some fair lady will wear this lovely pellage in America, and never once think of the jungle out of which he sprang, the countless murders on his list, the long dark hours of his bloody quest for prey or the tragic end of this beautiful and terrible beast.

Having measured the body, rolled up the skull in the skin, we placed it in our car and turned in search of fresh adventures. As we worked down the "spruit" or dry gully across the veldt, we saw at a distance how the vultures circled in the sky and the hyenas slunk off the plain and the herds of game parted into little groups, leaving a barren center where, lying in the tall grass, were three tranquil lions. We stopped and looked them over with the glasses.

There was an old monarch with a dark full mane,

and as he rested couchant, at his shoulder in a caressing attitude lay a young lioness. Off a few yards was a second male, young, full-grown, but beardless.

We drew near them in the car. The wonderful old male rose and gazed at us; his consort lay languidly at his feet. They were a glorious pair. The third lion seemed to have been the gourmand at the party who had done most of the eating. He was full up to his eyes.

They all started off at a leisurely trot. We followed and singled out the great male. Soon he stopped with an air of annoyance, his fat friend lumbered past him, and after a truculent look at us, reluctantly trotted off toward the hill. The young "flapper" seemed bashful and retired to the thick cover of the donga. We had the king of beasts alone on the open plains. He was a hundred and fifty yards off standing at bay, slowly weaving his graceful tail back and forth.

We all got out of the car and advanced together toward our lion. He showed no intention of running away, and every impulse to come forward.

We went slowly up to eighty-five yards and decided by his actions and low growl that this was just about his charging distance; another five paces and he would come at us with a roar and a rush. We set ourselves to shoot, adjusting our quivers for easy access to the arrows.

One flight and we got his range. We hit him, once

86

in the head and once in the shoulder. He reared and struck at the arrow in his forehead and savagely bit the shaft in two, at his shoulder. As he stood up on his hind legs and lunged at the shafts, he was a noble sight; a lion rampant! We shot again and drove an arrow deep in his side. With a snarl, he galloped off to the shallow donga behind him and stopped in the long grass facing us. He was now two hundred yards away. Here he roared and challenged us to come on. His gorgeous mane stood erect, his blazing eyes we could see through the glasses, but his restless desire to charge was visibly checked by a sense of weakness and pain.

We decided that the wound in his side was fatal, if we but waited. So we sought to avoid a charge and withdrew to the car. He lay down, occasionally raising his head to threaten us and growl. We decided to patch an inner tube of the automobile where a thorn had punctured the tire and thus occupy the time while waiting for the end.

At the expiration of half an hour, the noble old fellow had settled down and seemed nearly done for. We shouted and let an arrow fly at him. But he rose to his feet, sprang at the arrow and ground it in his teeth. Then as he stood there glaring at us in rage, he tottered and fell on his side. He lay with his head between his paws a long time, stirring only at rare intervals.

We waited, and then slowly advanced as a unit. He

gathered his fast waning strength and rose to meet us. We sent a volley of arrows at him, striking him in the head and chest. He sank to the ground, sighed a long deep breath and expired.

We drew cautiously up to him and viewed his magnificent body with wonder and admiration. One experiences mixed emotions on such occasions; triumph and pity.

We set to work to skin him and examine his wounds. His stomach was empty. His fat friend had done all the eating. The lord and master had devoted himself to the gentle arts of love. He measured 43 inches at the shoulder, was 112 inches in length, including the tail, and weighed about four hundred pounds. He was killed with three essential arrows, one in the liver and two in the chest, the rest were merely incidental. With all this sordid pathology, we viewed his fall with a touch of sadness, and though we took his life, we have written his name indelibly in the romance of the chase.

So we loaded his skin in the car and drove on.

On our way to camp we came across a family of mongoose, ran them on foot and shot three with our arrows for the museum. Later we landed a Tommy for camp meat, while Simson gathered in a marabout stork and fox for the sake of Los Angeles.

That is a typical African hunt with the archers. As soon as we are in camp we start repairing our arrows, sharpening their steel heads or making new shafts, for

THE KING IS DEAD!

these lions seem to like to chew them up, especially mine, which have white feathers and gay red trimmings. It keeps us busy in between hunts making new arrows.

In the afternoon we develop our pictures or stroll down the river in search of fresh adventures, then return for a hot bath and supper. Our sunsets here are a notable event, and it is a state ceremony, sitting under the eaves of the banda and watching the glowing colors fade into dusk.

After supper of young wart hog or steinbuck, soup, potatoes and the ubiquitous Ikoma pumpkins, and a rice pudding, we sit by the camp fire and play soft music and look at the stars. At the advanced hour of eight-thirty we crawl in bed to get ready for another day with the bow in Tanganyika.

XI

BUILDING A BANDA

May 24th, 1925.

WITH the advent of the rainy season, we have had to give a thought to our thatched roof, and the process of repair was an interesting sight.

The hut in which White, Young and I sleep is an imposing affair for this country. It must measure eighteen by twenty-four feet, outside dimensions. The walls are made of upright saplings set in the ground, with long slim poles interlaced and bound with bark, and the intervening spaces filled with mud, plastered by hand on the surfaces. The walls stand about six feet high and besides one narrow door, there are several small apertures that could be considered windows, if one didn't know better.

The roof on this noble edifice, when we came, was too flat to shed water, so the head man, Mdolo, was instructed to take it off and put on another with a steeper pitch and overhanging eaves to protect the mud walls from rain.

So for several days, boys carried in from the grove

near the river long limbs of thorn trees, both yellow and black mimosa, and straight trunks from palm trees. These latter are put in the important structure of the house because they are not subject to rapid decay and the destructive action of boring insects. The thorn poles last only a few months, and one may find his house tumbling about his ears, due to the collapse of the supporting beams.

Besides these timbers, the natives brought bundles of long poles and the stems of palm leaves. Then as binding material they carried in many leaves of that plant we call agave, or Spanish bayonet, or sisal. These they split lengthwise into half a dozen strips. They constitute bandage like thongs, very strong and flexible. The bark of the thorn tree, they also loosen by pounding and ripping it off the tree. This is particularly strong. I pulled out some of the finer fibres of this bark and twisted them into a string, which I found impossible to break with my hands. It would make an excellent bow cord.

Having all this in readiness and a large quantity of long tough grass that grows down in the donga, they set to work removing our roof.

A gang of twenty boys attacked our domicile, under the energetic supervision of Mdolo, and as they worked they sang. It seems that no important event takes place in Africa, that singing is not a necessary concomitant. They chanted a monotonous drone, varied with shrill interjections of accentuated phrases, and never ceased during the entire operation.

Part of their song seemed to be well known and stereotyped, then there were novelties introduced in the verses as some burst of musical genius took possession of the theme. They sang in Wakamba, or Wassukuma dialect and not in Swahili, which is the universal dialect that is gradually making its way in the multitude of tongues. It was somewhat of a surprise to us to find that these natives did not care for our sort of music. They paid no attention to it. I think they use an entirely different gamut from ours. One form they have is very interesting; it is an instrument made of a bow and a gourd. Quite a little harp like melody can be plucked from it.

At last the end poles with crotches at the top, were set in the ground, the long palm ridge pole was hoisted in place and bound there. The slanting rods that constitute the rafters were lashed to the ridge with withes of bark. Across these saplings, stems of palm were bound in a net work with sisal and after four or five hours' labor, the sort accomplished by many hands and minimum effort, the roof was ready for the thatch.

Bundles of sweet grass were tossed up to men on the roof, and these were spread out in a thick mat upon the basket work of saplings. Some rows of thatch were bound down securely with bark strips. Others were simply laid in place from below upward. When

they reached the top, the grass was spread across the ridge pole and held in place with long withes tied together. This thatch is six or eight inches thick.

Thus in one day was our house reconstructed. To test their work, the next night Dame Nature sent a good shower of rain and proved their work well done; the roof did not leak a drop.

In preparation for the wet season, several other little bandas have been built for the men; one in particular is interesting in design though miniature. It has a flat roof and a veranda, composed of palm leaves covered with clay. This they say is a good type to shed water. We call this hut the "Gunbearers' Club," for here our boys hang out and discuss past safaris and their many Bwanas and the doings of the day, and the size of the various game heads and the lions they have met. These gun bearers take a great personal pride in the prowess of their masters.

We were careful to get Wakambas for our men, because this is a tribe that uses the bow, and would have a patient understanding of the limitations of archery.

In this past week, though we have not hunted much, because of exploring safaris that were necessary, still I have personally missed so many good shots at game, Grant's gazelle, Tommies and wildebeest, that I feel deeply humiliated.

An archer like a golfer must think of seventeen different things before he can make a good shot. Just yes-

93

terday I made a stalk on a Granti and got within sixty yards. Now ordinarily one should trim the tail off a rabbit at that range with the bow, but my arrow flew a foot over the gazelle's shoulder, and a second one, as the startled animal leaped, then stood again to look, went a hand's breadth too high across his flank.

It is inexcusable! I remembered fifteen of the essential points: my stand was good, my back muscles were taut, my right elbow held level, my left arm rigid, my release firm and straight back, I drew under my jaw, I did all but the last two essentials: I did not draw completely to the barb of the arrow, and I did not focus my gaze on one single spot on the animal.

As we look at game, we nearly always overestimate the distance, and we focus our vision on the back contour of the beast; this is the most prominent outline.

What a bowman seeks is to make a heart or chest shot. He should rivet his gaze on the axillary fold, just back of the animal's fore leg. There lies the heart. He should not only forget back, head and horns, and look at that crease, but he should pick out an individual hair on that spot and try to split that hair.

This game is like golf:—one hurries on to that "next time," when he is going to do "everything known to science." Then his foot slips, or he plucks the bow string, and the whole day is spoiled.

94

XII

HUNTING METHODS

May 26th, 1925.

YOU will get "fed up" on lions if I don't stop, but we are still at this feverish business of hunting them, although I believe we can soon rest, because Leslie Simson departs tomorrow for Nairobi, thence to India to try his hand on tigers. Simson is our master of ceremonies, but life is too tame for him here.

Young and I may go after them with the bow and White can back us up with the artillery, but this leaves a good deal of responsibility on the shoulders of one man. Two guns are better and they don't always stop the beast. The departure of Leslie Simson is a distinct loss to our party. His experience and accurate shooting were invaluable. He has slain more lions than anyone in Africa. The actual count, of all sorts and conditions of these animals, is two hundred and thirty-seven, but he does not credit himself with more than one hundred and seventy-six, because some of these were females or immature and shot for museum purposes.

This is an incredible number, and no one in the hunting fields has anywhere near this count. Lord Delamere was considered a great lion hunter and he never quite reached fifty. Selous, one of the most picturesque and successful African hunters, had shot not more than half this number. Nor was Cunninghame credited with any greater list. Both these men, though great hunters in their day, devoted most of their time to elephant shooting.

As I recall it, Roosevelt shot something less than a dozen lions himself. From this you can gather that Simson is preeminently the great lion hunter of Africa. He is by birth an American but he has lived in Africa for thirty years.

And he has lived to shoot these many dangerous animals because he has set rules of action. Other men shoot a few lions, then get careless and a lion ends their career. Leslie Simson proceeds with his hunt along certain definite lines, and will not depart from these for the sake of glory or a trophy.

There are several well recognized methods of getting these beasts. In Kenya Colony, where lions have become more nocturnal because of continuous hunting, the most successful method is to build a thorn boma or ambush, lay a dead zebra or Kongoni outside at a distance of ten or twenty yards, then wait for simba at night and shoot him by flash light. This is not considered the most sporting type of shooting, but nine-tenths of all lions killed by visiting hunters are shot this way.

The next method is that of still hunting or tracking. In competent hands this is a very sportsmanlike and successful method.

Ordinarily, the hunter, well backed up with one or two experienced white hunters, hired for the safari, goes out early in the morning and looks for "kills." These are detected by seeing vultures in the sky or roosting on trees or on the ground near the carcass of an animal recently mauled. Hyenas sitting around or laboriously dragging their gorged bellies over the ground, are another infallible sign of a "kill."

Now the hunter must find the lion. If it is early, he may see it moving off in a leisurely, lumbering way, or he may find him lying under a tree near by, or in the grass of the donga, or he may see him a couple of miles off resting on a hillside. Here a powerful field glass is a great aid.

When the lion is located, then he must be approached. Lions do not run away like deer or antelope, still they move out of the country when they see man. They neither like his looks nor his smell. You may have to follow for many miles. Generally it seeks cover or a safe retreat in a kopje or an outcropping of rocks. But having at last come up to him, possibly having run him on foot for a mile or more till he turns and stands at bay, ready to charge, then you shoot.

97

Generally this shooting distance is between one and two hundred yards. At the longer ranges you may simply wound him, and he then escapes to hide in dense cover. Here your real difficulty begins. To get him out is dangerous and often impossible. To go in after him, you should be armed with a death certificate. When he does come out, he generally comes out at close range in a rush, and you shoot for your life.

When first hit, if not too far off, he will charge about once in ten times. If he is no closer than a hundred yards, here you have a chance to get in two or three shots, if you are quick. It will take him about six seconds to cover this distance and be on you, and you must hit him in the right spot too.

Another method of securing lions is by what is called "coursing," or running them with horses. This is great sport and preferred by most hunters where the country is suitable and where one can get horses. Unfortunately in most parts of Africa, a horse does not live long on account of the various infectious diseases transmitted by insect bites.

Having discovered a lion the horsemen chase him one or two miles, keeping a hundred yards or more behind him and off to the side, so that when he stops, the man on horseback does not run on top of him, and thus come within his reach.

The brother to Lord Grey lost his life by disregarding this rule. When you have him bayed, then the procedure is to dismount and shoot at such a distance that you have time if need be to remount and escape a charge.

There is of course the Massai method of spearing, lions, but this has not yet become popular with Europeans.

Here in the wildest parts of Africa, in Tanganyika, "coursing" by horses is impossible, because the tsetse fly and his trypanosomes kill the horses before you can use them, but the "fliver" takes the place of the horse here as elsewhere. It is moderately immune to sleeping sickness.

We are two hundred and forty miles from the nearest vestige of civilization, in a position that takes six weeks to reach by foot safari under the most favorable circumstances, yet we reach it, at least Simson does, by motor car in three days; and we can take out the old "Lizzie" and chase around after lions.

Mind you, we are probably the only people in Tanganyika that do this, and it is very unlikely that it can be done in any other place because of the absence of lions or the lack of suitable ground. But here we have rolling prairies and an unlimited supply of *felis leo*.

So Lizzie takes the place of a horse in Africa. Not all of Simson's lion hunting has been done this way. The vast majority of his simbas were shot on foot after miles and miles of walking and running, but in the past two years he has employed the car as a convenience.

99

It must be driven by an expert and one that knows lions, a sort of chauffeur difficult to pick up on the spur of the moment.

He must have an eagle eye for badger holes and hidden ditches. Racing lions is extremely dangerous. From what I've seen of the game, it seems quite as dangerous to run after them as to come up to them.

I shudder when I see Simson make his hairbreadth escapes from pitfalls missed by a foot, that would wreck the entire party. He speeds along at thirty to forty-five miles an hour, courting disaster while he travels, and running boldly into the jaws of a lion before he jams on the brakes, switches off the "juice" and hops out from among the pedals and levers with his big gun in his hand.

We all unload at once and are on the ground ready for business in a second. But sometimes we don't get a chance to get out, for the lion comes at us pell mell!

Just last week when Young and I were with Simson, we saw six lionesses saunter out of a donga where they had been on a kill all night.

We set out after them and by the remarkable generalship of Simson, we cut out one from the bunch and coursed her with the car. Inadvertently we ran too near, less than thirty yards, expecting her to continue a wide circle she was making. I was standing on the running board ready to hop off and land an arrow

SKINNING A LION

into her, for we have found that this stops them as a rule and they stand from then on.

She wheeled and came at us in long leaps. We swerved to escape her charge, and as the car veered sharply away from the lion, I nearly was flung into her jaws, holding on to the seat by one finger and having a most eerie feeling of swinging far out with no assurance that I ever would swing back again.

I saw the lioness over my shoulder and she looked like a running cat about to pounce upon a ball of worsted. I imagined I could see the fillings in her back teeth as she opened her jaws. I just fastened the rest of my digits on a substantial portion of the car and felt that I really was still going with the gang when I saw Young poke his Winchester rifle over the tail board and blast the lady in the face.

She was just one jump too short. That spoiled another bow and arrow trophy, still I felt there were compensations.

In the absence of White, Young was doing double duty: an archer when we attacked, and a gun man when the lions attacked us.

White was off in another direction filling up his own trophy list with the rifle. His interest in archery has been supplanted by his desire to get past the fifty lion mark.

We had another disappointment the other day. We rounded up a good sized male lion, selecting him out of a group that would have done credit to any animal act in a circus. We brought him to bay in the tall grass of the plains at half a mile from his boon companions, and there we assaulted him at a distance of some eighty yards, with our arrows.

Now hitting a lion at eighty yards, as he lies head on in the grass is not an easy thing with a bow. It is about the same as hitting a coal oil can at the length of a city block. And after you hit him you have not done him much damage, even with a bullet, much less an arrow, because he is so heavily armored by bone in his head and masses of muscle in his shoulders.

But what does happen when we send an arrow whizzing and strike him in the forehead or in the wide open mouth: he rises and turns, throws himself, rears in a most dramatic way, trying to dislodge the offending shaft. Then we shoot to get at his heart or chest cavity. We did this with number twenty-five.

Three arrows struck him in the head. Two went through his face and entered deeply into his throat. White was using his seventy-five-pound bow. He let fly a shaft that struck in the shoulder and buried half its length in the lion's chest. It was a deep wound. This coupled with several more hits in the body slowed him down. He would not charge, and after fussing about for a few minutes savagely tearing at his wounds and crunching the arrows near him, seemed to be sick or despondent.

We did not appreciate the gravity of his physical condition. We should have waited as we have done before when we were sure that a fatal wound had been delivered. But because we wanted to stir him up and ascertain his status, Simson shot at him with his twenty-two calibre rifle. No one imagines he can kill lions with a "twenty-two," or if he does, he would not continue to have any imagination after he tried it.

The little pill struck the lion right in the jugular notch. He was desperately sick, only waiting for an excuse to die. That little pill struck in the soft center of his neck, skidded along the windpipe and entered the heart. He flopped over on his side and gave up the ghost. I picked out the bullet when the autopsy was in progress.

I also picked out White's sharp broadhead deep in the pulmonary blood vessels, a quick and mortal wound.

But there is another trophy that should have been ours by all the rules of archery, that we can not honestly claim, all on account of a measly little twenty-two, shot just for fun, as it were.

However, we have done very well so far. In six weeks' hunting, we've seen one hundred and seventy-six different lions, killed twenty-four and five of these were dispatched entirely with the bow and arrow.

Most safaris consider themselves very successful when they get three lions in three months' hunting, but few have Leslie Simson to show them how.

XIII

THE ARCHERY CONTEST

June 7th, 1925.

THE past week has seen the arrival of the Ikoma archers, natives from the nearby village whom we invited over to visit us and show us their method of hunting.

They were delayed nearly three weeks by an important tribal ceremony. This apparently follows upon the rite of circumcision of the youths of a certain maturity, and as Hassani, our interpreter, explained: "They pray to the bush, and go without food for many days, and they dream and see visions, and they are given a man's name."

This sounds much like some of the adolescent ceremonies of our American Indians.

At any rate, the Wassukuma are real archers. We had two delegations: one a scouting party sent out by the Sultani to report on the game conditions around his territory. These were bearers of an official document written in Swahili; the Sultani has a scribe. The

message was to the effect that these men were his official representatives, sons of the elect of his kingdom;
they were not hunting with the bow; and it was his
royal request that they be permitted to pass through
all alien domains.

Simson's principality is recognized as a co-equal prov-
ince with which diplomatic etiquette is to be main-
tained with proper dignity.

We gave them bed and board and sent them off in
due time with salutations and rare gifts to the Sultani
of Ikoma.

The second contingent of archers came as a body-
guard to Masheki, the Crown Prince; and on the way
they incidentally took a shot at two maned lions "en
passant," just to show who was who.

So we have had the pick of the profession. White
says that they are the best bowmen he has seen in
Africa. Their bows are five feet six inches long,
are very strong, pulling about eighty pounds when
drawn the full length of their arrows. They shoot
farther than any aboriginal bows that ever came under
my notice.

Their arrows are well made, properly feathered shafts,
measuring thirty inches to the fore shaft. This latter
is a spindle of wood or a metal point, set loosely in the
end of the shaft, and smeared heavily with poison.

From their description of the effect of this "dowa"
apparently it is very similar to *curare*, or South Ameri-

can poison. Its action is very prompt; the animal runs a short distance, gets weak in the legs and stops breathing within quarter of an hour. They cut out a piece of flesh about the arrow and have no compunction about eating the rest. They gave me quite a quantity of this poison, which I hope to have analyzed later.

We offered a prize for the best long distance shot with bows. I entered the competition. Young has gone to Nairobi with Simson to bring back the automobiles. White has a sprained wrist and can't shoot a bow at present. So I had to represent the European peoples by myself. Half a shilling and a small toy elephant constituted the first prize, a little carved monkey the second.

They all shot, elevating their bows high in the air, then drawing full to the chest, with three fingers on the string, in what has been termed the Mediterranean release. Lowering their bow arm with too flat a trajectory, they loose the shaft and the sinew bow string gives a great twang as the arrow darts forth on its flight. Their arrows are much lighter than our standard hunting shafts.

Their longest shot was two hundred and forty-seven yards, according to White's paces. This is nearly fifty yards farther than any native bow shot, of which I have any personal knowledge. On my second trial I was able to exceed them by twelve or fifteen yards, with a very light bamboo arrow that I keep just for such events. I also out shot them using their own arrows.

We gave the prize to as fine looking, grinning, enthusiastic a savage as one could see in a picture book.

I also gave each archer a toy balloon, one of those that has a squawker in it. It tickled their fancy greatly.

What I have seen of their accuracy in shooting leaves me with the impression that they are quite a bit more haphazard than we are. I don't think they count on hitting anything past ten or twenty yards, save in mass shots. Apparently their system is to shoot into herds of game. Either the animals have been run together by fire or by native beaters, or by natural crowding as they migrate. Here is where long distance shooting is of value. Even a trivial wound means death to the animal.

We kill most of our large game at distances between forty and eighty yards, and never use mass shots, except in an African herd, where we were trying the experiment of finding out how large the holes were around each animal. Now that we know, we have ceased, for the same reason that should restrain a gun man: one wounds but does not kill.

I got the best of these Ikoma archers to shoot at our target. It is a straw mat three feet in diameter, having a six-inch bull's-eye, and set forty yards distant.

The average Anglo-Saxon hits such a bull's eye with

half the number of arrows shot. One boy, Selezia, with his native outfit, struck the straw mat twice, with six arrows, and missed the bull entirely. His arrows had a very poor flight, and tended to flirt or dodge during their progress.

I then handed him my bow and arrows and he hit the mat four times with six shots, two of which were close to the bull's-eye. "Shooting at rovers," or field shooting where one picks out a small bush or other natural object at varying distances for his mark, this boy was quite my equal.

So we arranged to go hunting together; three Wassukumas and myself.

Their methods of hunting with bow and arrow were what I wanted to see. Both Arthur Young and I have hunted with the Indians of America and know their system of getting game. The Wassukuma have a vastly different type of game to deal with and a much different sort of country in which to work.

My archer friends tried long distance shooting, and tried creeping up dongas to get closer to game, and tried running after game, either to intercept its mad rush to escape or to run it down and shoot at close quarters.

This latter method interested me particularly. It was a surprising thing to see two natives take after a Thomson's gazelle, one of the fleetest animals alive, and run it down. They circled and cut off and jogged

A NATIVE ARCHER IN ACTION

along where the gazelle wore itself out with wild racing. In less than one hour, they had the gazelle by the hind leg, when it sought cover in the long grass.

The natives do not pay as much attention to the wind in hunting game as we do, but they are very quiet in their approach and upon several occasions we were able to get very near to Topi and zebra, which are counted among the most wary.

They never seem to shoot at birds, for the simple reason, I suppose, that they never have shot straight enough to hit them. Other African natives however do use bird arrows at short ranges and get feathers for their headdresses.

Several times when hunting with these archers they called my attention to a little gray bird that was twittering and chattering on a nearby tree. This was the honey bird. We followed him as he flew from tree to tree, the boys whistling softly. Soon he led us to a bee tree. Four successive times we followed honey birds, and each time we found a bee tree. Later we chopped open the hives and secured very nice combs of honey. We always left some for the bird.

Upon one of our expeditions we were making a stalk through a rocky kopje and suddenly came upon a great python about eighteen feet in length, slowly creeping through the grass looking for something to strangle and engulf.

We shot it with our arrows, pinning it to the earth, and as it lay writhing I approached too near, when in its contortions its head shot forth and seized the crepe rubber sole of my shoe with its hooked fangs. The natives were greatly alarmed and called to me to beware of its tail, that it would encircle my neck and strangle me. I struggled vainly to free my foot, then I jerked out my hunting knife and cut its head off, leaving the huge reptile in a very detached frame of mind.

While this is not a snake country, we have seen quite a number of cobras, or black mombas, as we crawl through the deep dongas, for not only do we have to contend with thorns and tangled vines, but we must be forever on the lookout for the deadly cobra and the treacherous leopard. Stalking has its drawbacks.

Also our stalking leads us into the lair of the lion. In our hunting we have slain so many male lions that we have left a large number of bereaved and indignant females about.

On one of our trips with the bowmen, we came across two of these widowed queens in the thorn brush. Before I could restrain them, my three archer companions took after the larger lioness and started her on a run across the open plains. She fled reluctantly, and from time to time she turned upon the pursuing archers and switched her tail and made as if to charge. It was a critical situation, because they were armed only with their bows, not even a spear, and I was in no

THE HEAD OF A WILDEBEEST

position to assist them. On they ran with their sandals flopping, their long black legs flickering over the veldt. It was with deep satisfaction that I saw the lioness outdistance them and disappear in the jungle.

When I came up I remonstrated with them and said that we were out to shoot water bucks and not lions. I turned them from the cover and we went our way.

This did not altogether sink into their brains. They had heard that we killed lions with our bows and they were not afraid. Later on as we were trying to approach some zebra near the river bank, we saw the familiar complex which surrounds Simba. There were the vultures sitting in the tops of the trees; there were the waiting hyenas and there were the herds of startled game standing stupidly in rows and looking reproachfully at a recent kill.

It was perfectly obvious that lions were in the tall grass, within less than a hundred yards. How would you feel if you knew that lions lay in cover just over there, and all you had in your hand was a couple of sticks and a piece of string?

But these natives waded into the jungle with as much assurance as if they were going to kick out some grouse.

In an instant there was a rough angry growl. I called to my boys and they ran to me. I saw the head of a lioness less than fifty yards off in the grass.

We all ran close together and I motioned to the

111

Wassukuma to mount a nearby tree, a suggestion which they rejected with a scornful look. So we stood together, waiting breathlessly, our bows drawn, and I said to myself: "Now you are in for the real thing! This is a mess!"

And as we turned and stood abreast in a line of defense, the lioness took our challenge and came at us with a roar. My heart was jumping all over my insides but we stood firm waiting a close shot. We knew that arrows can't stop a charge, but we would do our damnedest.

As she came in those long sinuous leaps straight at us, she had to cross a small patch of tall grass some twenty-five yards off.

When she got there, in about three jumps, a miracle happened: *She stopped!* It just shows the power of thought. I thought she would come on, but she didn't. No, sir, she stopped! I suppose that the suggestion of cover and the appearance of four men, added together, were just enough to turn her intention into momentary caution.

As she stood irresolute lashing her tail and coughing out her rage, three other lionesses appeared in the jungle just behind her. All of them focussed their vision upon us, and seemed twitching to come.

One's ideas are very misty at these moments, but I had enough cerebral activity left to say to the boys one of the few Swahili words I know, "Rudi!"

("Back!"). And very slowly we drew away from too intense a situation. The lions watched us until we were eighty or ninety yards away, then they turned and disappeared in the donga.

I knew that I fell, in the estimation of three Ikoma boys, right down to zero.

But after all I am no lion tamer, I'm just a peaceable archer.

XIV

A LEOPARD MAULING

June 9th, 1925.

SOONER or later the man who hunts the big cats of Africa gets mauled or killed by them.

Leslie Simson has the greatest record on lions, but he has not as yet met his Waterloo. He is cautious.

A series of fifty lions is considered about the limit that a man can meet and conquer, and come off with a whole hide.

I told you that White was out to fill his list up to that limit. Well, counting his leopards, he has passed the fifty mark, but he has not done so unscathed. He was mauled three days ago.

The reason I have not told you sooner, excepting to send off a brief cable, was that my surgical practice has picked up so much in the past week that my literary activities have taken a secondary place. Two gun bearers were mauled at the same time. This is how it happened.

To begin at the beginning I must begin with the lions.

114

A LEOPARD MAULING

You see we have pretty well cleaned out the male lions from our immediate neighborhood. That is, we have shot some twenty-five of the one hundred or more that we have seen, and the rest have followed the wildebeest out of the country. One only is in evidence.

Of the old residents, consisting of several groups of indignant females, there is one band that we call the ten foolish virgins, because of their lone estate and their foolish antipathy toward us. And there was one particularly melodious lion that nightly came roaming over the veldt sobbing and roaring and grunting and parading back and forth just beyond the confines of our camp. He lived in what Simson called his photographic preserve and had his picture taken with a camera many times.

Because he roused the whole community with his deep resonant bellowing, we called him Caruso. And he had a musical harem with him. We had seen a couple of his female companions and had heard them snarl and beat defiance with their tails in the early gray of the morning, as we left camp on our hunting trips.

But no one had ever seen Caruso by daylight. He always went to bed early. His main function in life was nocturnal singing. He had a shy retiring nature.

White has been laying for Caruso's hide. After many unsuccessful forays into the enemies' country, about a week ago he met up with his quarry.   Caruso was just a few minutes too late in reaching his apartments.

White saw him and popped a bullet into his hide. The lion jumped into cover and lay "doggo." Around and around the gun bearers and White circled the bush.

Suddenly a patch of yellow in the jungle grass streaked past him. White fired and struck, but it was not Caruso; it was his large female companion. She dove into the donga, and silently awaited developments, and nursed her wound.

Now no hunter cares much to shoot females, in spite of the fact that a lioness is a more dangerous beast, and one of the worst of the game destroyers.

But White wanted Caruso. At last, by stooping low and peering under the matted cover, he saw him lying head on in the center of the thicket, about five yards away. A shot that centered his body ended the career of this lion. He was a fat old boy, who never did any work. His harem did the killing and he did all the singing.

But now there was a wounded lioness in the donga, or ditch or gully or shallow stream bed thickly covered with vegetation, whatever you choose to call it.

They threw stones and shouted at her, daring her to come out. She refused to budge, nor would she indicate her presence in any way. After a while, they sent a boy to camp to get native porters to beat the brush, shoot off firecrackers and bang on petrol tins; but she would not respond.

Then White did a very unwise thing, something that in his books he has deprecated and termed most foolhardy: he crawled into that donga to look for that wounded lioness.

He met the lady face to face and blew out her brains at short range. That was lion number forty-seven!

Lady luck was with him till he met this last leopard.

A few days later White said: "Well, we have been hunting pretty steadily for the past two weeks, and I think I will lay off and take a rest. I'll take just a little walk up the river to see where the wildebeest have gone."

Just a quiet little walk, it was to be!

He took along two gun boys: one for his heavy rifle and one for the twenty-two-calibered gun, also a couple of porters to carry home what camp meat or specimens he might shoot with the small rifle.

I went out with my native archers, looking for water buck. When I returned to camp near noon, White had not yet come in, so I lay down to rest my feet. In the midst of one of those tropical "forty winks" I was roused by the tent boy who brought my boots and said: "Bwana White wants you. He has a leopard wounded in the bush and one of the boys has been scratched on the head."

I thought he wanted help in beating the leopard out of the grass, so I gathered a half dozen boys and took my bow and my bag of emergency dressings as an afterthought, and started off behind the messenger.

We "hot-footed" it over the midday veldt for a long four miles up the river, when lo and behold, I found White and his two gun boys beneath a tree and everybody covered with blood from head to foot!

The Bwana was pale and weak and had one useless arm tucked in his binocular strap. Without a word I went up to him to inspect and dress his wounds, but he waved me aside and said: "Take care of Solomani, he is badly hurt!"

Being brought up in the army, I did as I was told. Solomani, the gun bearer, was lying in a coma with his head at the base of the tree.

Great gashes in his scalp and face, his eye gouged half out, his forearms deeply bitten,—he was a mass of shredded flesh and blood.

I set to work cleaning and dressing his wounds. White had rubbed permanganate crystals in them and those of the other man already, and afterwards taken the few remaining crystals and disinfected his own lacerations.

When finished with Solomani I attended to Kysuma, whose lesions were less extensive, then I was permitted to fix up the Bwana. I syringed all the deep incisions with a strong solution of permanganate and did them up in gauze saturated with the same. Thank goodness, my emergency dressings were just enough to go round!

Then we made a litter of long poles, coats and belts and carried Solomani to camp, White and I leading the way. While we were doing the rough surgery some of our boys went down into the donga and got the body of the leopard. They skinned it as I worked.

As we journeyed home, though weak and weary, White told me how it all happened.

It seems that at the end of their morning's walk up the river, they saw a leopard's head in the grass.

Just as White had drawn a bead on it and was taking up the slack in the trigger, the beast jumped. That fraction of a second spoiled the day.

As it leaped, White took a snap shot and hit it in the abdomen. As usual, the animal plunged into the thick vegetation. Here the hunters threw stones and shot the small rifle vainly trying to rout it.

For more than two hours they beat about the bush or waited for results. Then they decided to wade in and kick the rascal out.

A leopard is so quick, so vindictive and can hide himself in such short cover, that he is an extremely dangerous adversary in the grass.

Solomani and Kysuma, the gun bearers, went ahead and began treading down the tangled weeds.

Suddenly out of the very center of the bush arose

the leopard and landed sprawling on the body of unfortunate Solomani.

They were down in a second, rolling over in the tangled vegetation, partially hidden from White and struggling for life. All the time the poor man cried, "piga bwana, piga bwana"—"Shoot, master." White could not shoot from his position but ran as fast as possible to the scene of action.

The second man, Kysuma, was near and in an opportune moment discharged the little gun at the leopard. This saved Solomani's life, for the enraged beast now sprang upon Kysuma and fastened his fangs in his arm.

In this action he exposed his body and White shot the leopard in the chest.

Again the insane beast turned and with ears flattened and his cruel yellow face in a desperate snarl, leaped at White, dashed aside his gun and bore him to the ground.

Over and over they rolled until the man grabbed the beast by the throat, and, as he clenched his right hand about the windpipe, he drew up his knees to protect his abdomen from the hind claws and to force the leopard beneath him.

The struggle was brief. The attack with claw and fang lessened, and White felt the animal grow limp in his grasp. What with his gun wounds and asphyxia it soon lay dead under the body of the man.

THE GUN BEARERS

As I write, the Bwana is up and about, his wounds healing; the two gun boys are "doing as well as can be expected under the circumstances"—as the doctor always says.

When Arthur Young comes back from Nairobi, we shall lay in energy for further conquests and adventures.

But I shall nail upon the wall a homely old motto. Let me see! Here is one: "Every cloud has a silver lining." No, that doesn't fit!

Here's another. "Waste not, want not." No, not exactly.

Again, "What is home without a mother?" That's good, but not just right.

Oh! here it is. "Discretion is the better part of valor!" That's fine!

XV

A STROLL UP THE RIVER

June 20th, 1925.

HUNTING is a good deal like the description of a sham battle given by a raw recruit. "Fifteen miles of walking and fifteen minutes of shooting."

The actual shooting done with the bow, on one of our morning walks, is surprisingly little. It is true, of course, that the archer has one advantage; he can practice as he strolls along, and we often start the day with a dozen or more tentative arrows, to get our muscles in proper coordination for the real test.

Having selected what bow we want for the day, and having sharpened every broadhead in the quiver, and buckled on the arm guard and slung the quiver belt over our shoulder, we are ready to start the hunt. One or two natives, armed with bow and arrows or a spear, and carrying our canteen, camera and emergency surgical supplies, are ready to accompany us.

Dawn is blushing violently as the naked sun appears

over the horizon; the birds are chipper; the gazelles leap about in the dewy grass or stand gazing at us in dazed innocence as we file out into the land of adventure. We do not talk, partly because of the lack of a common language, and partly because this is the immemorial custom of hunters. The human voice carries a long way.

Now as a hunter walks along he has plenty of time to think and he must observe everything. Some men are natural born trackers, and their eyes are never off the ground: they seldom see game; others are landscape critics and see only the pictures before them; but the keen hunter looks at every object as though it concealed game or was game or had something to do with game.

If a man is only part hunter and quite a large part nature lover, he gets more out of his expedition than what falls to his bag. This is particularly necessary if he be an archer, because his bag will be small, though his enjoyment may be large. I must admit that the bow is more a companion in woodland pleasure than an engine of destruction; that's one reason why we like it.

So we sally forth to archer land, down the swale, along the river bank, through the wet tall grass and soon we are threading our cautious way in the maze of tangled vines, reeds and conglomerate vegetation. You would think that getting wet to your waist in this rampant verdure, might be unpleasant; but it is not, there are so many compensations.

If you are sensitive to delicate odors you find delight in the fairy-like fragrance of the grass in the donga. Very few of these plants have I been able to identify by sight. The faint aromas are ephemeral and intangible. Some flowers exist: I've seen the convolvulus and a delicate sweet pea, and the tiny blossoms of the mimosa tree, and orchids high up in the overhanging palm leaves, but there are more than these. And as they are elusive to the eye, so they are correspondingly exquisite to the sense of smell; they are elfland incense.

And how often have I wished I were a botanist, a geologist, a comparative anatomist and an ornithologist.

These very grasses entrance me. There are so many. Some I seem to recognize: bunch grass, buffalo grass, marsh grass, elephant grass, tall and like bamboo. The common grass of the veldt looks like Bermuda grass, with long vine-like runners or suckers, and growing with it is a dry dusty grass having tall stems supporting masses of tangled linear leaves, looking more like a snarl of thread than anything else. Wild oats are everywhere and couch grass and sorrel and clover and familiar weeds whose names I do not know. In great profusion in certain areas the deadly nightshade, or belladonna plant, grows in some places to the size of small trees, while in the thickets stand the dagger-like sisal and aloe blades, ready to wound you should you enter. And every bush seems to carry a thorn to puncture or incise your flesh. But these we learn to avoid and ignore.

As we steal through this botanical garden, we see the small life of the jungle. Birds of dazzling yellow and blue or slim green frogs that leap high out of the matted undergrowth and land yards away, always toward the river.

Perhaps you suddenly drop into a deep wart hog hole, and thank your guardian Fate that your joints are firm, your bones well calcified and your ligaments all gristle and tough.

Down in the bed of the river, which now stands in brackish pools, sometimes slowly trickling over volcanic bed rock, but deep in shadow and cool, you creep upon a water buck who stands breast-high in lush grass, feeding unaware. Now there is a beautiful beast in this land of ungainly creatures! The water buck is truly admirable; of splendid proportions, something like our mule tail deer but chunkier. His horns are long and curved slightly forward, his pelt is thick and dark brown, his gait is graceful and swift when need be. I like him! But he is very wary. As yet we have not landed him with the bow.

Down in the donga we creep. A mud turtle slips off a log into the turbid water, further on a slinking hyena shows his spots through the thick screen of leaves, and

I let fly an arrow at him. It sounds as though I hit the loathsome beast and he vanishes in the jungle, but then I find my arrow buried in the mud bank. I overshot the mark. There are always hyenas down in the thick stuff, and leopards too, but they are more alert and we seldom see them. Sometimes we do, but you recall how one treated White just a little while ago. We don't like them!

We creep along, avoiding the detaining thorns, stepping on the succulent turf where we can to prevent noise; setting obstructing limbs carefully aside, by hand, crawling through the tall cover where the river bed is shallow and ever feeling for the cool index of the wind.

An eland, a lone bull, appears near a game group and we include him in our calculations. One of the natives, Selezia, a tall handsome fellow, crosses the water hole and circles to get behind this animal; my way is blocked by a large open space. Selezia stalks him well and I see him crouch to shoot. His silent arrow flies from sight and the startled eland fades into the universal green of the tropical stage.

We go on as the archer runs forward to get his shaft. Later he shows me where he struck in the hard bone of the leg and bent his arrow point: a mere incident to the eland.

On we go by winding paths where the crumpled weeds indicate a reed buck's nest, and soon a flash of dark orange, a leaping gleam of golden light and the reed buck has bounded with infinite grace beyond the harm of our long bows. So quick, so supple, I've never seen such an animal before!

One of these beautiful little deer can be lying down, in the deep grass, with its legs curled under it, looking innocently in surprise at your strange appearance in his domain. You draw the bow string to shoot, and as the arrow flies, and before it can strike, that beautiful little creature has bounded into full stride, with no intermediate movements, and is hurtling through the jungle with extreme grace and rapidity. If you are a good shot, you hit the place where she was.

It is a shame to say it, but twice Young and I have anticipated this nimble escape.

Along the river bank the monkey families live. These comic caricatures of man are exempt from our molestation, but they are an unending source of delight to us with their dare-devil leaps from tree to tree and their "fire escape" exercises. In spite of the fact that all these trees are bristling with thorns, these little gray, long-tailed, solemn-faced mannikins hurl themselves from incredible heights and grasp a branch of this thorn tree to check their fall, glide down a drooping limb and land upon a tree across the river, and never once seem to indicate the presence of thorns. I don't know how they do it!

Six little wistful, large-eyed lemurs sat upon a bough

and watched Young the other day. They are so timid
and harmless they seem to trust all the world with
implicit faith in its kindly intentions. They were not
deceived in Young. He let them scuttle off to their
jungle destiny.

Wild Egyptian geese rise from the water pools and
wing their squawking way to some nearby tree, where
they invite a flying shaft, "fledged with a gray goose
feather." So far fortune has favored them!

Herons, blue and white, vault into soaring flight
from shadowed depths of the donga.

Storks with pink bills and snowy wings teeter and
balance upon the topmost limbs of the yellow thorn
trees while solemn and stately marabouts stand in
formal conclave at some post mortem consultation in
the glade.

Spurfowl whirr off beneath our feet and sometimes
get a startled arrow swift from the bow, yet too late
to intercept their rush.

And so the morning goes. The sun climbs higher
and strikes us through the clustered palm leaves

It is nearly time to turn homeward.

We search another patch of cover; one path leads
to a further, and there is always the possibility of fresh
adventure over the next rise of ground. There we
do find it; lurking in the cover we see what we mistake
for a reed buck. Selezia and I both shoot. His arrow
strikes what proves to be a young water buck. It

SELEZIA—MY HUNTING COMPANION

runs, we trail and find it. We shoot again and finish the job. We load the little calf on the shoulders of another native boy and start him off toward home.

By the time we reach camp we shall have walked ten or fifteen miles. With the pedometer to check us, we often travel twenty to twenty-five miles in a day's hunt. So we rest on the stream bank and unstring the bows and let the cooling breeze blow in at the open collar and watch the tumbled clouds drift slowly through the faultless blue. Vultures wheel far up in the sky, the cicada sings in the branches overhead. Tanganyika is a very lovely place!

Then we start for camp. Part of the way we retrace our steps through the more inviting portion of the river shade, on the chance that we may flush a few more head of game from cover, and failing in this we strike out across the open plains in a direct line home.

Even here there are things to be seen: shifting herds of game; perhaps a taunting Tommy invites a shot, and cleverly dodges our futile shafts.

We pass a mound of rocks near two mimosa trees, out in the center of the valley. I ask the Ikoma boy what it is. He says a great Masai chieftain's grave. Then following an ancient custom he reverently picked up another stone and places it on the mound, as though it were a flower. We journey on; with legs that take up the problem of transportation and leave the mind free to contemplation and repose, and thus at last we arrive.

Having come to camp, and being after luncheon, it is my duty as surgeon of the outfit, to dress the wounds of Bwana White and the two gun bearers who figured in the recent leopard episode.

White's wounds in shoulder and arm are about healed, and one gun boy is well on the road to recovery. But Solomani, the other gun bearer, is in a pretty bad way. The wound made in his orbit by the leopard's fangs is a destructive one. Fragments of bone and dirt were carried in back of the eyeball and made their appearance later, accompanied by quantities of pus. The eyeball itself was wounded and is now a useless and infected body. His deep incisions in the arm look like shrapnel wounds and are infected with trench bacteria, so that the whole condition is a rotten mess.

Our surgical equipment is limited of course, and we are taxed to the utmost in ingenuity and resources to meet the surgical condition. He is improving, however, and has no septicemia. The eye is a complete loss and probably must be removed as soon as the orbital infection subsides. In spite of all this the brave fellow smiles at White, on his morning calls, and says: "Bwana, I shall soon be good again, then we will go out and shoot another lion." That's the stuff that Swahili gun bearers are made of.

XVI

SUNSET IN TANGANYIKA

June 27th, 1925.

THE day is done. Two more lion skins hang in the palm leaf banda of the skinner; the tension and the throb of the chase are past.

Now we sit here bathed and subdued, watching the day fade over the low level horizon of Africa.

Evening comes as a benediction in our camp. Replete as the days are with adventure and excitement, it closes the scene of each diurnal phenomenon with a profound and satisfying experience.

The chill of the upland plains is just suggested in the vagrant breeze, and the camp fire before our thatched grass hut is a welcome addition to the setting. Supper is yet to come and we rest in our canvas camp chairs, in silence and blissful contemplation of the sunset.

It is a daily religious ceremony.

There is no doubt about it: we are Pantheists here. No pre-occupation takes precedence of this great farewell performance of the day. We view it in rapt attention.

Sunsets have been considered banal by some, and many sunsets do strike a commonplace note in their pyrotechnics. But in Tanganyika their charm is unsullied by stereotyped effects; gaudy lighting; overplayed dramatic pauses.

The scene here starts reluctantly. Great billows of dense smoke like vapor gather above the western rim and obscure the sun. A mood of melancholy droops over the heavens and life seems poised in indecision and doubt. The canopy overhead is still that pure azure of faultless ether. Immeasurable distance extends above, and space itself is non-existent.

There is no hint there of change.

But at the level of the eyes are sullen clouds, a recalcitrant solar orb, and the dimming of color intensities that forebode decay.

Below the level of these tumbled billows of smoke, a transition occurs: the blue that was, that darker tint which gathers at the edge of the firmament, descends a degree in the spectrum, and is by magic a pastel green of the very faintest verdure. A strange thing, to see a green sky!

Stark against this background of incongruous color, stand the low hills with their flat top mimosa trees; and over yonder at the very side wings of the stage, beetles the shadowed profile of Kuba Kuba, the lone mountain of our landscape.

Now all is in readiness for the hero to appear. He

does so! Hot and naked in flame, the sun dips a sector of its periphery below the curtain of dusky clouds. It is blazing copper, large and imminent. One feels its turged, inflammatory emanations, as if the defiance of the shielding earthly moisture of the low hung screen, excited it to more ardent function.

It seems to drop across the intervening area of clear heaven and strike the edge of the earth like a burning meteor.

Vanished is the pastel green, and in its stead a most delicate lavender background surrounds this fulminant sphere.

The dense curtain above, now no longer murky and leaden, has changed to dove color, soft and gray. It is not thick as it seemed, but translucent and flocculent.

Across the gentle undulations of this texture, gay and roseate blushes seem to pass with delightful uncertainty. The clear space below it, burns with greater heat; all the elements of blue have been consumed and in their stead, dazzling incandescence takes their place.

Then as though a furnace door were flung open, the whole heavens burst into flame. All moods and pathos flash into life and passion. A gigantic conflagration sweeps over the sky. Driven as by a mighty wind the flames of destruction leap from crest to crest setting each afire with its torrid intensity. The whole celestial universe is a mass of intolerable radiance. It is turned to molten gold; consumed in infinite glory.

A moment too tense to last!

There is a pause: imperceptibly it fades. The gold turns to brass, the blinding flame to yellow; the very atmosphere seems to precipitate into scintillating atoms of cooler light. This haze of solar crystals grows thin and ephemeral and leaves but the afterglow of a great reaction.

Life gravitates to a lower level.

The clouds above that but a moment ago were inflamed with ardour, now look demure and even pallid. A fading blush still lingers on their gentle contours, but listless and detached in mood they float apart. They appear more diaphanous than before.

The sun is gone. Like a spirit of necromancy his place is filled by an after image of vacuity. The stratum of light at the horizon seemingly has an aperture where but a second before, there stood the miracle of light.

Wan shades of spectral color, drawn like thin veils of mystery above the silhouetted sky line, merge in depth of tone and constitute the background.

The pale anæmic clouds above, disperse in languid hesitation and show but fleeting waves of warmth, as though a memory of their past splendor.

Evening is here and night casts a shadow on the scene.

134

STORKS DOWN BY THE RIVER

SUNSET IN TANGANYIKA

As though the sun had never been, the day is cold and gray and chastened.

Stillness rests upon us.

And so it is over! One's soul is steeped in beauty and the quiet heart is flooded with a surge of gratitude.

The breeze wafts a faint fragrance from the wet jungle grass in the donga, and twilight pervades all space with its intangible calm.

Down by the river pools, sounds the low rasping cough of the prowling leopard and the herds of wild game gather on the open plains for safety.

The night wind rises and fans a dozen African camp fires before little grass huts, where the hum of mellow voices and native laughter float upon the air.

The stars come out and over there in the ominous shadow of Kuba Kuba rumbles the distant bellow of a lion: muffled grunts followed by a roar, then a sobbing decadence. It casts a momentary spell of silence over the earth.

For a space we do not breathe.

So the vast illusion of night descends upon us!

Thus sets the sun in Tanganyika.

XVII

AN ESSAY ON THE WILDEBEEST

July 1st, 1925.

THE wildebeest, or Nyumbo, is our most prevalent game animal hereabouts. You may recall him to memory when you know that he is the familiar "gnu" of the circus menagerie and zoo.

To all appearance he belongs to the buffalo family and does not look unlike our own American bison. In size he is a trifle smaller, lighter in limbs and has straight hair on his neck and shoulders in place of the mass of curly wool found on our bison. His horns are heavily bossed where they are attached to the head, and curve in an outward then inward sweep, quite gracefully. His head is long and rather narrow. A Roman nose marks his profile which is spoiled by very flattened nostrils. He has a beard, thick neck, sloping shoulders, small hindquarters and a mule's tail.

His color is a rich dark brown; his long hair is black, with chin whiskers of yellow or gray, and his general expression is one of sadness and stupidity. His running gait is a stiff-legged gallop, very ungraceful but tireless. He can travel for miles without stopping, and in spite of the general awkwardness of his appearance his speed is phenomenal. They say that even on horseback, one has difficulty in catching up with a wildebeest.

I know that a "flivver" can't run one down.

There is, however, something in common between a "flivver" and a wildebeest. Their singing voice is about the same. The wildebeest blats like a sick tin fish horn, and so does the "flivver."

These wildebeest when in numbers, give forth a chorus of laryngeal vibrations that would be in perfect euphony with the squawking one hears in an automobile parade at "Pumpkin Center," during a County Fair.

All night long when the great multitudes of these beasts are about our camp, we hear the incessant, dismal fog horn of their complaint. They seem to be saying, "lion-naw," "lion-naw," "lion-naw!" The eternal dispute between the timid and the doubting Thomas of the herd.

It seems that they have good reason to harp everlastingly on this one subject, for it is the usual thing to hear them go stampeding across the plains running here and there in the dark as they are harassed by these great cats. All night long they congregate in the open spaces trying to avoid attack. They circle

and whirl and stream off in a long single file, then
bunch again and all "present arms" to the enemy;
their horns lined up in a phalanx of defense. In the
day time they do not seem to fear lions so much. And
we have often seen lions in their midst, not more than
twenty yards away, and yet beyond a watchful eye,
these herbivora pay little heed to them.

Once when we were chasing two lions trying to
bring them to bay out on the velt, a herd of wildebeest
rushed in between them and us and so obscured the
field with their incredible numbers and the cloud of
dust that arose, that we lost our quarry in the
shuffle.

At another time these animal morons insisted upon
gathering in a wide circle directly back of three lionesses
that we were preparing to assault. There they stood
like a crowd of innocent bystanders ready to get shot
at the first fusillade.

However, we paid scant attention to them, we had
other things on our minds, and a wildebeest more or
less out of a herd of ten thousand meant nothing in
our young lives. We would have added his meat to
the morning's bag, without scruple. He is in fact our
regular camp meat, and to feed our forty or fifty men
we supply them with wildebeest at the rate of three
or four a week.

When we want potio, or ground maize, from the
neighboring native village, we now send them dried

138

wildebeest in exchange. One animal is equivalent to four bags of potio, sixty pounds each. And his tail has a value of two shillings or half a load of meal. The whole animal on the hoof appears to weigh some five or six hundred pounds. Of course this makes about a quarter of this weight in dried meat. It is a picturesque sight to see a caravan of natives start out for Ikoma with their bundles of dried wildebeest tied on sticks over their shoulders.

I can't say much for the native methods of slaughtering these animals after we have shot them. They cut them up with their crude iron knives in a most outlandish manner, and after a preliminary amputation of the creature's legs, the rest of the operation seems to lack rhyme and reason. They seem to have no idea of interior anatomy and the niceties of sanitary technique. They hack it to pieces and smear up the beast in a most unbecoming way so that no white man would eat of it.

I suppose they think it adds to the gamey flavor. Since we have many Mohammedans in camp we must be very careful to have each beast properly "chinzo"—or stuck in the throat with a knife and bled by an authorized disciple of the Great Prophet, or the entire carcass is a complete loss: they will not eat it. Happily these Mohammedans are not over scrupulous about making a diagnosis of death. Any beast that has not undergone rigor mortis is still counted alive in their opinion. So long as the blood will flow a little, it is all right.

But the wildebeest alive and in his collective numbers is much more interesting than dead.

In some portions of the game fields of Africa, this animal has become so scarce, that to see a hundred in one herd would be considered a great sight. They do say that in the Kadong valley, in Kenya Colony, a favorite resort for all big game hunters, there is one lone wildebeest who bears a charmed life and that countless boxes of ammunition have been expended upon him, while he, most elusive ruminant, whisks his tail, turns a few spiral loops, kicks up his heels and cavorts away over the boundless veldt.

Here in Tanganyika the wildebeest is no "rara avis." When we heard that fifty thousand of these creatures were located permanently in the volcanic crater of Ngorongoro, we were ready to make that difficult journey just to see them. But here in our very midst we find ourselves at times entirely surrounded by the beasts.

We go out after lions in our palatial Ford truck and ride for hours through vast multitudes of them. We have tried to stay conservative and still we estimate that in one little valley some ten by twenty miles in diameter we have seen no less than a quarter of a million wildebeests. They look like flies on sticky fly paper in a cheap restaurant. It is incredible!

The pictures that old timers on the American plains

gave of our herds of buffalo are paralleled by this African cousin. In fact they have become a nuisance. Too much game to do much hunting. Anyone who wished to study the mob psychology of gregarious animals would have a wonderful opportunity here.

They seem to be organized into groups or family herds, each governed by a field marshal, an old bull, whose business it is to keep the gang together; to lead them in their rushes and military maneuvers and to protect them against intrusion.

This old warrior romps back and forth alongside the herd; hooks any straying cow, and charges any meddlesome bull of another group or one of those secondary in rank to himself who comes too close. There seem to be a number of younger progressives always on the outside of the bunch that would like to lead, but "*haven't got the* guts" to depose the old man just yet.

Then there is always the old worn out chieftain, a dower lonely outcast, who hovers on the outskirts and broods gloomily on the past. Things were done better in his day! His conquests on the field of glory and in the gentle art of procreation are a forgotten glory. He is an embittered old "has been" and usually stands apart under a tree or off on an ant hill and sulks. This is the dangerous rogue that hunters do well to avoid. We see him in all animal groups, even lions have their deposed monarchs. In the elephant species this type of beast is especially dangerous and to be shunned.

Animals in Africa breed at all seasons, and consequently there is no "closed or open season" for hunting. So we see young wildebeest calves of various ages in these bands. They are especially amusing to watch as the herds go through their erratic gyrations on the field.

We may be traveling quietly along in our car, when a band of these foolish animals a mile off will decide to cross the line of our progress. There is no need for this maneuver. We have not frightened them: we are not intervening between them and a desirable section of ground. Simply one curious old cow gets an idea, first that we will bear watching, she wants to see what and who we are, and so she starts in our direction. Then some leader of the faithful swings into the front and charges across the prairie in our direction. With a thunder of hoofs and a cyclone of dust they bear down upon us. Sometimes they line up in an abrupt halt and gaze a moment, then about face and make off in great haste. More frequently they string out in a thin line and race across our bows. Faster and faster they go: the last individuals of course have the hardest time as we crowd them, so the utmost speed is expended by these belated fools. They swing out in a widening semi-circle and strain every nerve to accomplish this great desideratum. The little calves often wind up the rear, and such running you never saw! They outstrip their seniors; their little legs just

WILDEBEEST ON THE MARCH

flicker in the vibration of flight. I am sure they reach a speed of fifty or sixty miles per hour, and maintain it for a half mile or more. When they at last all get by, then what do they do? They wheel about and stand and look at us, and just as like as not, if they get another chance they repeat the process and chase back whence they came; such curiosity and stupidity!

As an experiment, Young and I went out on the plains at night with a lantern and a flashlight. The mass of beasts at first retired as we advanced. Then they circled around us and as we drew near, they disbursed. Again they collected about us and closed their ranks. I flashed their eyes with the electric lamp and in a whirl they ran up to us with gleaming orbs and heaving dark backs. So close they came that their wild vortex nearly engulfed us and one foolish heifer ran directly against our light, only swerving at the last stride, and spared us an unwholesome experience.

Their reaction was a mixed one: timidity, curiosity, defensive tactics: blind bewilderment and fear. We discontinued the experiment and went back to camp.

We have not hunted these prosaic beasts very much with the bow and arrow, but in a recent excursion we came across a native camp and saw the fleeing occupants running off with their archery equipment, their few personal possessions and what slabs of meat they could carry flapping all about them as they ran. We saw their pot of meal and meat stewing on the embers,

143

and wildebeest hides on the trees, and we left the scene without disturbing the situation. They were successful hunters and we approved of their occupation. There is a recent law dictated by the English Government which prohibits the native from hunting, with the object of making him agricultural. It will be about as successful as prohibiting the average small boy from going swimming: it is foolish prohibition.

Poaching added to the spirit of the chase makes the game all the more desirable.

No, we have been too busy with lions to devote much time to wildebeest, but we have made enough observations of the habits of these creatures to know that it is difficult to shoot them with a bow. Their great numbers are a protection, and while we can approach them within a hundred yards with the car, as soon as a man steps out and on to the ground, they are off like a rocket and a quarter of a mile is the distance they consider safe.

The old misanthropic bulls that stand and sulk under the trees are our meat. Here we haven't a thousand watchful eyes upon us and we can make a successful stalk. Or we use a blind near a water hole, though this is not very sportsmanlike with the gun, it is all right with the bow and arrow.

We are not bent on murder of many of these simple minded quadrupeds; it is too unexciting.

So far we have slain only three with our arrows and

144

these trophies of head, horns and whiskers will stand in evidence of our ability to bring them low should we care to.

As it is, we leave them soon with our blessing, knowing that they will go their guileless way and blunder on to their own destiny, as food for innumerable lions.

XVIII

THOUGHTS IN A TREE

July 4th, 1925.

THIS is the great Fourth of July, and as true Americans we have celebrated it appropriately here in the British Protectorate Colony of Tanganyika.

The Stars and Stripes float over our camp. We started the day by setting off three firecrackers, some of the supply with which we scare lions out of cover. Then we went out and twisted the British Lion's tail, three times, that is, Bwana White and Young took a long ride in the national car, the car that made America famous, and after locating another camp site some twenty-five miles from here, where the wild zebra and the wilder wildebeest roam the plains in great abundance and the wild grass is extra plentiful and wild; after locating all this they met up with five lions and bagged with the guns two, and as they came home in the afternoon they met an old lioness just outside the camp that had not had a square meal for two weeks and tried to take a piece out of the car, so they shot her and brought her home to help the celebration.

146

Then we wound up by taking a zealously guarded piece of pound cake that had been brought all the way from London for the event, and found that this English cake had turned rancid at the thought of our national independence; so we contented ourselves by playing "God Save the King" followed up by two chasers, "The Star Spangled Banner" and "Dixie" —played by the full orchestra—three in all—count 'em!

But the past week has been a quiet one, we have hunted lions and brought home quite a number of skins. They have, however, not been shot with the bow. In fact I doubt that we shall shoot any more of them with our honorable old weapon. White is not willing to take the responsibility of backing us up with the heavy artillery. He contends that it is too much of a job for one man. I guess he is right. We have had some close figuring, and just one mistake in judgment would mean turning the tables on the hunters, something that is fair enough all right, but there are the women and children to think of, to say very little of the distressing personal inconvenience of being mangled by a justly indignant lion.

Just at present we are working on the blind problem: shooting from blinds up in trees, at game that cannot be approached by any other means. In many ways in this African hunt we find ourselves defeated in our preconceived plans of procedure. Where we considered the abundance of game a favorable factor in securing meat, we find that this very abundance militates against our success. We stalk a waterbuck by a manœuvre that should be successful, and four reed buck and two dik diks jump out of the grass ahead of us, where they were hidden. They so startle the waterbuck that our half hour of careful approach goes for nothing and the opportunity has vanished. We make an early morning hunt for topi, one of those large antelope, and after five or six miles of walking, we come upon a suitable group for a stealthy attack. We get down in the dry donga and laboriously crawl through thorns and jungle grass, only to find that a bunch of Tommies on the opposite side of the donga has winded us and scampered off over the plains and put the entire game field in a state of commotion. We lose the topi.

Birds protect a large number of game animals and they are forever piping forth their warnings to some favorite beast. The rhino has a regular crew of tick birds that perch on his ears or horn or eyelids and feast upon his pendulous ticks. When these busy-bodies see a man they soar aloft and squeak their notes of warning so that even this sodden dunce is aroused to apprehension and lumbers off "into the blue." Giraffes are walking ladders for gay little fowls that run up and down their necks and never seem to leave their host. These also act as informants and gossips.

THOUGHTS IN A TREE

The hornbill, a large magpie sort of a bird, is a great hand to trumpet forth the glad tidings to all the animal kingdom, "A man has come to town!" Waterbucks especially appear to have a ready ear for this type of scandal.

The lack of cover; the inconstant breeze; the flat monotonous skylines; the crackling dry grass, twigs and volcanic stones, all combine to defeat the enthusiastic archer. So we look more and more at the native methods with approval. They are not ours and never can be. We rebel at the use of poison, though it is utilitarian if not sporting. We scorn to shoot into herds of game, but they don't; and just a day or so ago we were watching a great drove of wildebeest running off through the scrub thorns, when right in their midst arose five or six native bowmen and followed among them shooting arrow after arrow into their midst. The dust and welter of the stampede aided them in this form of hunting. That's how they get their meat. Of course all their arrows are poisoned and even a trivial wound causes death.

I have tested out this "dowa" that they use, and find it very effective for the purpose employed. M'tone, the Sultani of Ikoma, sent me a segment of bamboo filled with this black tar-like poison. It is made by cutting up the limbs of a certain tree and boiling small chips of it to a thick gummy consistency. I took three frogs that we captured down at the river and

149

mixing about one grain of this "dowa" in a teaspoon of water, I injected about five drops of the solution in the hind leg of each frog. They all died in less than four minutes. The type of death seemed to resemble curare poisoning: that is there first came a paralysis of the voluntary muscles and the animals were unable to move; then respiration ceased while the heart action continued, and last a drop in blood pressure as indicated by the blue skin and distended capillaries of the tongue and web of the feet, which was followed by a fibrillating heart and complete cessation of life.

On each arrow shaft used by these natives, there seems to be as much as twenty grains of poison, and this they say is ample to kill any beast in quarter of an hour.

You often hear people say, "Be very careful of those arrows, they are poisoned," As a matter of fact, there is not a single poison used by natives that could harm you from a simple scratch. Even rattlesnake venom, one of the most deadly, would not injure a person from a scratch, supposing that the venom were then rubbed in the wound. It takes as much as five grains of crotolin, placed under the skin, to kill a man. Strychnine is much more concentrated than any poison used by natives. Even supposing that this were rubbed in a scratch, no harm would result. It would take at least a grain hypodermically to produce death.

ZEBRA FROM A TREE BLIND

The South American natives use curare, which requires over five grains to be effective.

The natives of Central America use a substance exuded from the skin of toads, called Bufogin, which is very toxic. The Japanese aborigines, the Ainu, use spiders and the root of the aconite plant. I doubt that the spider has much kick in him when it comes to lethal dosage. He is put in the incorporation for the sake of his name; an influential personage. But aconite is a real heart depressant. The toxin developed from the tetanus germ is the most powerful poison known to man. A microscopic quantity is sufficient to produce death. Happily, this is obtainable only in the sanctity of a bacteriologic laboratory, not on the market.

So, deprived of these natural resources in our African game hunting, I am again sitting in a tree boma waiting for topi and zebra to come to the inviting water hole before me. As I wrote these words a fierce little blue falcon swooped down upon a linnet drinking at the pool and pinioned him to earth. Even at the risk of scaring a band of zebra that were this moment forming in line to drink, I rattled my arrow quiver and hissed at him while I dropped my pen to launch a feathered shaft. Alas, he was too quick, and flew away with the pretty little red top linnet in his talons.

Hardly had this episode passed, when out from a crevice in the rocks scuttled a large purple lizard.

He darted hither and yon, bobbing up and down with arms akimbo and his head was bright pink. In fact, his head and neck were luminous with an interior red glow, like a Chinese garden lantern. He was a remarkable sight. He scurried from point to point on the rocks, looking over his domain, and apparently finding it satisfactory, he changed his color tones to a dark gray, extinguished his luminous head and vanished under a large stone.

This morning I noticed that the flight of birds was disturbed with no visible cause. They did not pay any attention to me, though I am but half concealed up in the foliage. The doves and blue enamelled starlings roosted in the nearby tree and twittered their warning notes. After a long wait, two little weasels came out of the grass like little man-eating lions, bloodthirsty little villains. Soon after they went away disappointed, two longtailed slim-bodied mink came stealing through the rushes. I shot an arrow at these murderous hunters and frightened them off so the birds could come and drink unmolested.

Going home yesterday from the blind, I saw two beautiful golden-coated leopards stalking reed buck in the grass. There was an object lesson in quiet approach! Those leopards walked and looked and waited and walked a few paces and looked again, and never a rustle of the jungle grass, not a sound from their padded feet. Masters at the game! Cruel beasts they are! I am afraid of them. Nevertheless my native boy and I crept nearer and nearer, hoping to get a shot.

Slowly the male leopard sank in the grass and as he did so the female vanished in the yellow cover. Long we waited and watched! But quiet though we were, they saw us and when at last our patience was exhausted and we openly assaulted their retreat with stones, out jumped a cringing reed buck and the leopards had gone. When all expectation of seeing them had departed, a tawny streak, flashed past us in the tall grass and was lost in the donga.

I was just as well pleased. White's wounds are but now healed and the two gunbearers mauled in the last leopard escapade are just out of danger. So I guess it is as well that we did not come to an issue. But there was the challenge! And man is ever looking for excitement! Well, a leopard gives him all he's looking for, sometimes.

Those zebra stand out there in the fading sunlight with their noses up wind and their tails beating a slow rhythm to fly time. I don't know whether or not they feel thirsty enough to come drink from this pool of questionable water. But here come the flocks of sand grouse and pigeons for their evening drink, the shadows are getting long under the trees and the birds that have been silent start their vesper songs. A cool breeze wafts gently through the mimosa trees and Africa seems very peaceful.

THE ADVENTUROUS BOWMEN

Soon it will be time to unstring my bow, lower the quiver of arrows to the ground and wander back to camp in the afterglow. I have not slain a beast to-day—and yet I am content, more than that, for I have captured a hundred beautiful memory pictures of beast and bird and jungle life and shall carry them with me forever.

XIX

ELAND AND SABOKAKI

July 9th,1925

IN this part of Africa, the giraffe is our largest animal. There are but a few rhino and no elephants.
We have more rhino at the next camp we expect
to make, on the Grumeti River. Here I hope we can
have some worthwhile adventures with this cumbersome but dangerous pachyderm.

Next to the giraffe in size comes the eland, and a
noble creature he is. I don't know whether he belongs to the antelope or the buffalo family. But he
looks something like the cattle that constitute the
domestic cow of Africa, only he is larger. He is
larger than any domestic cattle of America, if I am
any judge; and an eland is very much better looking.

Small herds of these lordly beasts are found along
the river banks or near dry river beds. From six to
a dozen congregate together, but generally assemble in
military formation conducting their maneuvers with
precision. They are so formal that they look like
animals out of a little wooden Noah's ark. When

seen on a skyline they are often in single file, their fine straight horns tilted all at the same angle, their straight backs on a perfect level and they are equidistant from each other.

These horns on adult bulls are slim conical shafts having a corkscrew fluting running about the axis. They stand about two feet high and set at a slight angle backward. They are among the most symmetrical and well formed horns seen on African game, strong and well proportioned. The hide of the eland is thick, but with fine grained short hair. Its color is so much like that of a lion, sort of a tawny gray, that they often are mistaken for lions at first glance, before their size and other features become defined. Another character of their build that helps to confuse them with lions if one sees them in tall grass, thus obscuring their legs, and before the distance and size are correctly estimated, is the straight line of their backs.

Most African game seem to stand on stilts or have their foreshoulders higher than their hind quarters. This makes them ungainly in the main, sort of slumped. Except for the representatives of the deer family such as the impalla, and similar species, these tropical herbivora have not the grace and poise of our deer and elk.

But in spite of its size the eland is graceful and even agile. Though the neck is full and the brisket hangs

156

low and the legs are short and the trunk is ponderous, these creatures can jump like goats. When they are put to flight they gallop off with great alacrity, running at a speed of twenty to thirty miles an hour, and frequently leaping into the air like the cow jumping over the moon. They leap so high, they often go clean over another member of the herd. One of these eland stands five feet or more at the shoulder, so you get some idea of their athletic ability. Though I am not a good judge of weight in cattle, I should say a fat eland would tip the scales at fifteen hundred pounds. In fact, this hurdling of theirs is one of the best things they do. They have no fancy "get away" when it comes to the start of their sprint. They are not like the topi, Kongoni and Tommy, who turn a handspring and do two side twisters before they begin to run. An eland is an old-fashioned, heavy weight, long distance traveler. If you crowd him he throws on a burst of speed, but his fat tells on him and he soon gets winded. If you let him take his own gait, he can travel all day.

Nor is he difficult to stalk, compared with most African game. If you can get one by himself and keep a fair amount of screen between you and observe all the requirements of wind and sound you can get quite close. We have been able to come within forty yards of them on several occasions. This is very sure bow and arrow distance.

I am surprised that lions don't kill more of them,

they seem such easy meat. But as a matter of observation, there are comparatively few eland kills. The lion seems to prefer wildebeest in this country. Perhaps it is the flavor of the meat, perhaps it is because of the great herds, they can stampede these foolish creatures and in the confusion make a successful rush and bring one down.

The eland does not escape attack entirely, that is certain. The last bull that we shot for safari meat presented many deep scars on his rump, typical of lion claw wounds, and in addition, or subtraction, he was minus a tail. Only the stump of this invaluable appendage remained. Apparently the lion had mistaken the proper end for assault, or had made a tackle while the bull was in active retreat, and landed on the rear platform. His hold on the departing eland was too insecure to be effective. Perhaps he kept the tail as a trophy. It is a remarkable fact that we never see any young of this specie. I suppose it is because their breeding ground is elsewhere.

The eland is very valuable as camp meat; though we do not shoot many, his fat is the source of our culinary lard. Great quantities can be obtained from one beast. Two petrol tins were filled with fat, from the last bull, and only the trimmings were abstracted, no particular pains were taken to go after each rich repository.

The lobular mass of adipose tissue surrounding the

YOUNG PICKS UP A FRIEND

heart must have weighed twenty pounds, and half filled the five gallon container. The natives dig right in and cut out titbits of succulent suet, particularly at the base of the tail, and eat it raw.

The meat of the animal is among the nicest found in Africa. It is tender and sweet and has not a game flavor at all. Steaks of eland back straps would be all the rage in the gastronomic centers of New York, if they could only get them. Some day a wise and provident person is going to import eland and breed them for their edibility. They are easily domesticated, so 'tis said, and we have seen them ranging in perfect harmony with the little Masai cattle.

Mr. Percival, one of the best white hunters of Kenya, says that they had a tame eland bull on their farm, and it was difficult to keep him from living with the family; he insisted upon going whither they went and whence they came. At last he had to be presented to someone else: he was too familiar.

The long bones of the legs of this accommodating being are used for soup stock. I don't know of any place where soup is at a higher degree of perfection than in our Tanganyika camp. There is always a pot of it on the fire and one could live entirely upon it if necessary; it is so strong and sustaining.

And while we are revelling in these gustatory descriptions it is not inopportune to mention that the bone marrow from the eland, fried and served upon toast, would soothe the savage breast of the fiercest gourmand.

The hide of this invaluable provider is used to make sandals for the natives and leather thongs, or "kamba" with which our bundles are bound and the porters use as straps to shoulder their loads. The long fascia or sinew of the back muscles they take to bind their bows and make the cord.

So you see the eland is an ambulatory emporium of "eats and fixings," "gents' furnishings," too!

While these African natives have feet like rhinoceros hide, they have foot trouble even here in the jungle and their pedal extremities need protection even as ours do. I am being called upon constantly to treat minor wounds and injuries of their feet. What with long thorns and sharp rocks and saw grass, their poor feet are forever in need of repair. Hardly a man who hasn't lost a toe, or has deformed nails from infection, or suffers from what is called "veldt sores," sort of a saddle gaul on the feet.

So the crude protection of a sandal is strictly in order. They are wide and floppy, but they save the epidermis.

Of course the "Marididi" or dudes, the boys with safety pins in their ears and copper wire coils around their arms and little brass bells on their ankles and a string of china buttons around their necks,—these boys wear sandals of old "non-skid tires," or "Nobby tread" when they are obtainable. But they are the elite; zebra hide and eland are for the rank and file.

Now that I've sung the praises of the eland, it is a shame to say that we shoot him with the bow and arrow. Yes, Arthur Young and White and I are here to try it out on everything, except the human residents and their near relatives the monkey family, and we make exception to giraffes and storks and similar long-legged defenseless species. We haven't shot many eland; they are not the sort of game that one kills indiscriminately: they are not in great droves, and they are patricial in character. But to determine whether or not the arrow driven by our strong, effective bows, was capable of dispatching these large animals expeditiously we have shot them. We found that we could drive an arrow to the feather in their chest and reach the heart, and death was immediate. In fact, the arrow was so effective that in one instance where shooting an eland for safari meat, at long range, the animal's leg was broken, with a heavy bullet from one of our lion guns, I put the creature out of his misery, with an arrow in the chest, killing him in less than thirty seconds.

I don't believe the natives shoot many eland with their bows, because they seemed to think it a great treat and an unusual thing when I served them this product of our archery. It was "nyama mizuri" (meat good); they do love fat meat. Their favorite beast is the zebra. We can't see anything about a zebra that looks good, from his coughing bark of a bray to his yellow, greasy meat.

But then a wart hog is about as unprepossessing an animal as one could wish to see, and all the books on Africa classify him as the one meat that even a native won't eat. But our native chauffeur, Sabokaki, or "Kaki," for short, one of those oily skinned, big mouthed, musical voiced likeable sort of comedians; he is very fond of wart hog and about the only one who will eat it. Of course no Mohammedan will touch pig, and many of our boys belong to that religion. But Sabokaki is in his glory when we get a wild boar. He fairly oozes oily delight. We give the whole pig to him. Once we shot a little porker and decided to try him ourselves. We try all these animals, except the hyena; even lion meat we found tender and sweet; cheetah meat was clean and like veal; so we braved wart hog. The young one was delicious. By mistake the cook served some of the old boar's chops for dinner, and surprising event! the old wart hog was not rancid or strong—he was as good as roast pig at home. So we reversed our opinion on the subject of African pork and voted that Sabokaki was a lucky Ethiopian.

XX

A CONFLAGRATION AND A GUINEA HEN

July 12th, 1925

THE big head line stuff in our camp this week is the conflagration that occurred. Perhaps you have not heard of it yet. Two of the straw huts of the Wayumwezi boys have been "razed to the ground by fire,"—as they say in the "Punkin Center Journal."

The palatial mansions in question are built of little sticks and mud for walls, circular in form, and have conical straw roofs on them. They must measure eight or ten feet across, with the walls standing at least four feet high, and the roof is like nothing so much as a Palm Beach hat which has seen better days.

You see, two of the boys,—Cigaretti and Tumbo, were cooking their dinner of corn meal and meat over a little fire in one of the huts and took the opportunity to retire to the river for a bath. How they can build a fire and live in them in spite of the smoke is a mystery to me; and why they all don't burn up is a greater mystery. Well, while they were away the roof caught

163

fire and the alarm was spread. Such scurrying and bustle you never saw. I didn't see it either. I will tell you later where I was. But the town gossip has it that there was a great to do here in our "thriving community." At least two buckets of water, thrown from the basins and cups, were expended upon the conflagration. Sticks and stones were hurled at the flaming edifice, and in a masterful effort to save the real estate, they tore down the mud walls and brought the attack to a successful issue, after all combustible material had been oxydized.

Of course the adjoining residence became ignited from the great cloud of sparks. It was sixteen inches away. It suffered the fate of the unfortunate first, and given the same heroic treatment. To cap the climax, and really what made this a menace to the whole of Africa, a third structure became ignited. Yes, sir! The fire department was taxed to its last resources! And here is where real genius shines. Exigencies of this sort bring out the master mind.

When the straw roof of No. 3 Wayumwezi Avenue, burst into flame, someone, now lost to fame I fear, I was not there to record it, someone suggested lifting off the roof and setting it on the ground where they could spank it into submission. They did this. They lifted it off like the lid of a sugar bowl, set it gently on the ground and beat the fire to death.

When I returned I viewed the smoking ruins. But

A QUIET DAY IN CAMP

no one seemed dismayed: no one had lost any property. The two boys had their three yards of cotton cloth, all their wardrobe, on them, at the bathing resort. They also had their copper wire bracelets and their walking sticks. They hadn't even lost their dinner. Some provident bystander had rescued that. Nothing is lost in Africa!

By evening they had set the detached roof back on the circular walls of residence No. 3, and two or three boys more or less in one of these huts does not overtax the housing facilities of the place. The more the snugger! In a day or two, new buildings will rise where the charred skeletons of those magnificent edifices, lost in the recent holocaust, are now a monument to our great catastrophe.

While all this transpired, I was off hunting reed buck with the bow and arrow. Arthur Young and Stewart Edward White are away, you recall, chasing the elusive king of beasts, twenty-five miles distant, encamped. So Challo and I were off for a gentle stroll up the river, what we call the river: a series of isolated stagnant pools, which in the rainy season is a rushing body of water. Challo is my gun bearer. That is his official title, but poor fellow, he has had to put up with a good deal in this archery game. Instead of tenderly caring for an arsenal of heavy artillery, cleaning and oiling its metallic mechanism, I have had him sharpening arrows and packing a spear and an extra

165

quiver and a camera. He is a great elephant and lion tracker, and I make an archer's assistant out of him. It is humiliating!

But since White and Young have gone, Challo will not let me leave his sight, not even to step out and look at the moon, without tagging right at my heels and packing the 405 lion gun that my brother in Detroit wished on me for "safety first."

So Challo had the 405 over his shoulder. I submitted meekly, especially since we have two wounded gun-boys in camp and my white companions were all away, and nobody to give me a decent funeral. So we walked up the river, where the grass is tall and the reed buck bound off like magnified rabbits, and we get but a fleeting shot, but it is fun. And I had about determined we would turn homeward at the next bend of the river, when Challo hissed "Simba" in my ear, snatched my bow from me and thrust the 405 in my hands.

Well, I've shot a few lions with the gun, and a good many more with the bow, but I've always had comforting companionship. I am not a great lion hunter. I don't want to shoot lions all by myself. I am willing to share the glory. Having seen lions in action and talked lions for months, and heard stories of lions, at first hand, I've come to the conclusion that the mortality risk of the single lion hunter who is only a fair shot and inexperienced runs between twenty-five and fifty per cent. Practically all men hunting lions are backed up by one or two white hunters.

But there was Simba, a fine, big fellow, standing broadside at about forty yards. Thank goodness, he was across the donga; not that this donga would stop him when he started to come my way. But you know how it is in the "big open spaces, where men are men" —even a wagon track between you and a lion looks good.

Well, I am not going to tell you how I dropped upon one knee and held the bead of the rifle on his fore-shoulder and squeezed the trigger, oh, so gently. No; you can read that in all the African Big Game books, just how the "mighty hunter" did all this. I am not going to dwell upon the scene of the tumbling beast and his roars and how just then a second lion bobbed up out of the donga, unwanted, uncalled for, entirely superfluous. I had all the lions I wanted and would have been willing to sell him to any young and ambitious nimrod, cheap!

Yes, number two arrived. Turn the page in the "Mighty Hunter's Book." You will find just how I soaked him in the gizzard; everything just as they all do: it's an oft told tale and a little threadbare; you almost know it by heart. And then how he charged! But the rest is too awful!

When he flopped, I felt like doing the same. Why is it that the Mighty Hunter doesn't have a good prescription in the Book to stiffen up one's knee joints. But then I am no "lion man." I tell you right now, I came to Africa on a peaceful mission! And as I was coming home I took my honorable old bow and arrow and shot a guinea fowl from the topmost branches of a tall yellow thorn tree, a mighty good shot, and got more satisfaction out of it than I did when I followed the instructions in the "Mighty Hunter's Book."

But when we came to camp packing the guinea fowl and the boys carrying the lion trophies, old Solomani the wounded gunbearer, with his helpless arm and his one bandaged eye, must toddle out of his hut and shake me by the hand and say: "Bwana makuba": (Big Chief), so tickled over a couple of dead lions, he didn't seem to look at the guinea hen. Childish pleasure these people take in a little thing like that!

XXI

GRASS FIRES AT NIGHT

July 14th, 1925.

BWANA White and Young are away at a separate camp hunting lions and other fearsome beasts. I had to stay behind to look after the boys who were mauled by the leopard. Solomani has lost his eye completely and is badly disfigured about the face. My patchwork on his cheek and eyelid makes him presentable, but that's all. His arm is still helpless and deeply infected. The other boy, Kysuma, is about well and White, of course, is up and doing.

We have seen the hills ablaze at night where White and Young are camped. They have fired the long grass and miles of country is swept by flame. This is the customary practice at this time of the year and is not harmful to the game; they run around it. Later on it makes good pasturage for them. In a few days they come back and nibble at the young shoots of grass.

They sent in a truck today for more supplies and word saying they had added ten more lions to the list, and one rhino. All this, of course, is the usual type of hunting, there is no novelty or romance about it. White has definitely abandoned the bow and now is out to make a record on lions with the gun and he has taken Young with him to assist in the clean up. The rhino they got was too far off for Young to try his arrows on the brute, and there was no cover to permit a closer approach. After it was killed by Young, he tried some of his regulation broad heads on the hide. He writes that where they struck a rib, the points were turned, and where they did not, the entrance was five or six inches into the chest, and that a shot in the neck entered nearly a foot. It is too bad that he did not have his regular rhino arrows with him; these would do better, since the blades alone are six inches long, and would enter that much at least before any friction of the shafts occurred. Even that much of a hole in the chest would kill a rhino, or any other animal.

Our party has now bagged over fifty lions on this expedition and personally I feel that we are overdoing the matter. Others are coming after us. Mr. H. O. Harrison of San Francisco and party will be the first to enter here since Simson located this paradise of wild game. From now on many safaris will come. Though there are countless lions, apparently, we have shot enough, and I am in favor of shooting only those that are unavoidable.

So far as the bow and arrow goes, we have proved our point and for the time being have discontinued the experiment.

It does not seem that we shall be able to hunt with the Masai spearmen as we hoped. An unusual drought rests upon this part of Africa, and the water holes between here and the Masai camps are dry. We cannot visit their country, at Ngorongoro. This a genuine disappointment.

As for the rhino, that is a moot question. Young and I certainly shall give him a run for his money, if we get a chance, later on.

Having been left alone in camp with some thirty boys to keep in meat, it takes considerable of my time, on foot, chasing these crazy zebras and kongoni and topi over the plains trying to get within half a mile of them and bring home the bacon. I am tired of keeping my sights on the 405 raised to 300 yards. I am no sharpshooter and that gun was never meant to do long distance stunts.

But in spite of this I spend half a day strolling up the river bed or in the tree blinds with my bow. Here I scribble these epistles and watch the small game and occasionally get a shot at big game with an arrow.

This afternoon furnished a new African problem. It

is another demonstration how active competition is even here in the jungle.

My perch up in this particular thorn tree is a quaint little place, elevated some twenty feet above the ground, composed of a nest of cross limbs and a screen of brush, reached by a rustic ladder running along the trunk of the tree.

It is an admirable roost from which to observe game, take photographs and for the bow a legitimate blind from which to shoot. The water hole is some thirty or forty yards off and game trails lead in all directions over the veldt.

There are many similar water holes along the river, so we are not taking advantage of one of the necessities of game life. From eight o'clock and on, game come at intervals during the day to puddle in the brackish water and drink.

In spite of the elevation, the human scent is carried by the wind, as much as half a mile out on the plains, and game crossing the line of communication will stop and look, and usually turn away from the spot. Zebra especially are sensitive to odors, and since they in common with most game approach a water hole up wind, very few come near my retreat. Tommies don't mind the scent so much and stray around the blind all day, but alert to dodge any arrow sped at them. Other beasts wandering aimlessly in search of diversion stray past the blind or occasionally break the rules

172

A TREE-BLIND

and come in down wind. Then I get a shot, perhaps.
The slightest noise startles them, and many dry twigs
are incorporated in the boma, besides obstructing
limbs and small branches to divert an arrow.

So it is not all "candy" for the archer. Shooting
down hill at unknown distances helps to make the
results problematical, as they like to say in polite
society.

However an old kongoni, one of those sad-faced,
homely, horse-like antelope of Africa, strayed into the
field of action today. He nuzzled the water in the
distant pool, then he ambled over to mine. I saw him
coming, and got up on my knees in the nest, to get the
crackles out of the situation before he came within hear-
ing. Kneeling there in prayerful silence I let him come
over and gaze at the green scum on our pool, and as he
stood in sombre "thot," I slowly drew my arrow to
the barb and swore by all the patron saints of archery
I would not overshoot him, and I would hold on his
foreshoulder.

As the sharp barb of the arrow met my knuckle I
loosed the bowstring. The kongoni jumped, but this
time too late. The shaft struck his flank and buried
half its length in the body cavity. As if a leopard
had leaped upon his back the creature plunged, reared
and twisted. Then as though he would dislodge the
enemy by speed, he took out across the plains, and as
he swung around a curve of the river where the tall

173

reeds grow thickly, he passed behind the screen of foliage in the trees and was lost to sight.

Two hundred yards or so he ran, then look as I would, I could not follow his course nor did he appear on either side of the river lower down, nor out on the plains. I said to myself, "kufa," which in Swahili means, "dead!"

For quarter of an hour I waited, in the blind, when I heard a very strange noise just where I saw the kongoni last. It sounded to me like the cry of a baboon, an unusual quality it had. As yet I do not know all the sounds of the jungle, but it did not resemble the bleat of an antelope. So I gave it up, but determined to look in that particular clump of palms and reeds as I searched for my kongoni.

After half an hour I got down from the blind with my bow and slowly went over the ground, trailing the beast where I could in a very much trodden ground. No blood marked his route.

At last I came to the half acre of thick jungle grass where last I saw him. I waded cautiously through and about in it. No kongoni was visible; no baboons either. One particularly thick overhanging clump engaged my attention, and I stooped to scrutinize the arched grass over a run way. It did not look good to me, and I felt sure that the kongoni had not gone in there, so I passed on, explored both sides the river and scanned the wide panorama of the veldt.

He was not in sight. I went back to the blind to think it over, and perchance to get another shot.

After a long while I came down determined to explore that thick cover. I worked the reed patch over again then at the edge of the donga, where a steep bank was thickly hedged with buffalo grass and brush I started to force my way into this tangle, when right at my feet, probably less than three yards away, came a rustle of reeds and the sharp staccato growl of a lion.

I did not need to think. My reverse gears were already in action and at ten yards I stood with my bow drawn, waiting for the next act. Of course it was a futile gesture on my part, but it was the only one I had to offer.

Then I recalled that I had seen a couple of female lions near this spot a few days ago. They were lurking there yet!

No further sound came from the jungle and you know what I did: I turned with dignity and left them severely alone. I am out one kongoni, but I've lost no lions in the tall grass.

As I returned thoughtfully to camp, I saw three vultures sitting on a tree overlooking the spot. They are not waiting for me: not if I know it!

XXII

THE WART HOG AND TOMMY

July 15th, 1925.

YOU wouldn't think that in Africa it could be cold. But the mornings are really quite chilly at this altitude, some 5,000 feet above sea level. And I am sitting here now in my green leather coat as I write.

There are roughly three climates in Africa; one in a very hot humid area, thick with brush and bugs, near the coast; one jungle climate, swampy, hot and malarial; and this the high plateau climate, very much like California. So I sit here waiting for the rain to come, a little cold, in Africa.

A boy passes with a stick on which two petrol tins hang; he is on his way to get water for the cook. Another cheerful black is whistling and singing his native plaintive song as he chops down a tree near the river, with a primitive axe that looks as if it had come out of the fifteenth century. The sky is overcast and a shower will soon descend upon us.

Stretched out before me are the barren plains, calling for water, empty of the great herds of wild game that but a short time ago crowded their surface. Rather desolate is the whole setting. But Africa is used to desolation and drought. The game takes care of itself somehow, and the dry scorched ground of today springs into verdant plenty almost over night, after the first sprinkle.

One must take Africa as the natives do, without concern for the future. When game is plentiful and crops are good they gorge themselves, sing, and hold their native dance ceremonies; and when times are hard, they live on nothing, sleep and wait for something to turn up. And I've not seen an unhappy native since I came. These boys never fight or have quarrels. One reason: they have no alcohol. That is another reason why they stand the tropical sun so much better than the white man. The legend of the "vertical rays of the tropical sun" is largely perpetuated by the amount of liquor the tropical white man drinks.

From what I've seen of the problem, and I admit that we are not in an extremely hot area, but we passed through these districts, but from what I've seen of it here and on the Red Sea it is the "vertical drop of the tropical tipple" that gets these men. Dr. Anderson, who has lived in Nairobi for twenty-five years told me that in all that time he had seen only two cases that he could classify as "sun stroke" and in each instance the man was drunk.

I believe there is such a thing as heat stroke, or heat exhaustion, but there must be heat. I don't believe in the mystic, actinic rays that are neither hot nor do they effect photographic plates, yet on dim days they strike one dead, after a few moments' exposure of the uncovered head. That one must wear cork helmets and red woolen cloth next the body and hot spine pads over his vertebral column is "tommy rot." It has all the ear marks of the "evil eye" and "moon blindness" delusions.

We dress here as we would out West, and wear felt hats, ventilated. I believe any hat or clothing that would be suitable on our hot summer days would do admirably in Africa.

As for crawling around in those picturesque "shorts," trousers cut off at the knee, that you see in all the pictures of African sportsmen, that is done by the English Johnnies who come to Nairobi; go out on a short safari and shoot a rhino and get their pictures taken. They are not suitable for wading through brush and thorns and tall grass. Scratches and insects afflict you and ticks crawl up your legs. They are part of the African legend.

One charming Englishman, Rodney Wood, I met in America, where he was doing Boy Scout work, said that he lived in Nyasáland, south of here, and that he never burdened himself with all those trappings of superstition. He wore a simple cotton shirt, cotton trousers and a straw hat, and never felt the sun. He is also an archer, which is likewise to his credit. He used the native bow and shot many of the smaller animals of the country.

Simson also shot the bow, it must be remembered, before we came. He bagged a zebra and a water buck with his arrows, here in Tanganyika. So we are not the first. Of course our archery excites quite a bit of skepticism among the local whites; and in fact many small calibre hunters have sort of a cynical sneer for it, or treat it with alleged humorous ridicule. This is because it is a challenge to their "mighty hunter complex." They resent seeing the thing they have done, which they considered heroic, being done with simpler implements and with greater fairness to the game. Men of larger experience and a more intellectual viewpoint in sport, often give us the most hearty support, as witnessed at the farewell dinner in New York of the African Big Game Club of America. Here Mr. Arthur Young and I were treated most royally and given every encouragement and approbation in our enterprise.

But we are not here teaching sportsmanship, nor preaching the return to archaic methods of the chase. We are here in an adventure of pure romanticism. We admit we are quixotic. At the same time we have a

179

curiosity to see just where the bow stands in the scale of the "arms of man." And though its limitations often come in violent contrast with the highly developed efficiency of the modern rifle, and our shooting often is by comparison a futile diversion, a child of optimism rather than service, still the background of romance and honorable achievement rests with our beloved weapon. If we but chose to descend to the natives' standard of living, dress and sporting ethics, we could subsist here on the returns of our shooting.

In the past week, Selezia and I, hunting with the bow and arrow have shot a Thomson's gazelle, two guinea hens, a young waterbuck and a kongoni, to say nothing of another large python, which we rule out of the edible list, mainly because of psychic reasons. I have no doubt he is good eating.

Selezia is the fine Ikoma youth who has been hunting with me since Arthur Young is away. He brought his young wife over from Ikoma some days ago. An intelligent, alert young woman, dressed very "chic" in her well-tanned antelope skin, her beaded anklets and the wide ring of brass wire about her neck. This latter is characteristic of the Masai women rather than the Wassu Kumas. And Selezia looks Masai, so straight and fearless in appearance. So I asked Hassani, our tent boy. He said "Yes, the boys call him Masai and his mother once lived in that country," maybe; perhaps! Well, it is possible.

But these bow and arrow expeditions, I spare you the minute details of how we stalked the game and how we missed or how we shot and where we struck. The hunter likes to know just how far our shafts went in and what they hit and how soon the beast expired. But I spare you the horrible details and even myself. For with us, so much of the hunt is seeing the life about us, feeling the cool morning breeze; watching the play of color in the eastern skies and the deepening shadows beneath the jungle palms. It is all part of the adventure and we often spare the game as well and pass it with a stroke of the eye instead of an arrow.

It is such fun to see some of the jungle folk. Only yesterday I sat way up in my nest in the tree and watched the antics of three wart hogs that came on the scene.

They entered nonchalantly, even jauntily. Old Papa Hog with his ivory moustaches, long tusks curving fiercely upwards like the Kaiser that was; his bristling pompadour brushed back; Ma with her inquisitive nose twitching at the end, her side whiskers of white bristles, and their adenoid child, very stupid mentally I am sure. Suddenly mother gave a grunt and wheeled about: "Something is wrong; things are not as they should be!" Dad takes the case in hand, perks up his snout and whiffs the air: "Yes, there is something rotten in Denmark!" He tries the breeze this way, then looks searchingly with his little shoebutton eyes, then gets down on his knees and seeks for a clue on the ground. He sniffs audibly. Of course it must be on the ground: all things are of the earth, earthy!

Ha! He has found a clue! No, he hasn't! Ma twists and turns and makes suggestions. Little Adenoids looks more like a moron than ever. He is going to be just like Pa some day. A baffled look takes the place of curiosity. That most exclusive family, the great Wartywarts, themselves, have been affronted. They now look haughty and distant. To think of it: "Somebody has been here at our summer resort; we, the wartiest wart hogs of Hog Town!"

Just then I loosed an arrow at old Colonel Warts himself. His suspicious nature served him well. He heard the flick of the arrow crossing the bow, and had a convulsive seizure in which he revolved on one hind leg, dug his toenails deeply into the ground and beat it just in time to escape a cloth yard shaft.

And such undignified scurrying! The Wartywarts were never in such a hurry before. With grunts and squeals they scratched gravel till distance lent enchantment to the view. Then with their ludicrous long tails with bristle tassels at the tip standing straight upward from their southern exposure, they trotted stiff-legged off the field of encounter, haughty and insulted! I nearly fell out of the tree laughing.

'Tis endless delight to watch the gambols of the

gay little Thomson's gazelles. These pretty little creatures the size of a small goat, but infinitely more graceful, congregate in small herds, that merge at times into multitudes. But just now a few dozen constitute the bands. Each of these is marshalled by a captain, or old buck, whose long curved horns and general air of superiority denote "Who's Who." His business is to dictate the going and the coming of the flock, to keep order, to be a squire of dames, when that shall be necessary, and mainly to keep any young upstart from getting his job. Then there are the lesser bucks who tend the flanks and act as scouts and outposts. These busy males spend most of their spare moments in holding jousts and tourneys, affairs of honor. There is a veiled threat, or an insinuating look and two rams come together with a click of their little horns, a flurry of dust, a strategic withdrawal, a menacing attitude, perhaps a repetition, and then a chase of the psychologically inferior, or a truce, pro temp.

There are the juvenile males, with budding horns, jaunty actions, incredible agility and a knowing little toss to the head. Soon they will be the "Big Chief," "then they will show 'em how!"

The females are in about equal numbers. The young dams run in small cliques, skittish and coy; sometimes singled out and pursued by an ardent male, fleeter than the wind they lead him on, generally to disappointment; then return waggishly to the bunch and "tell 'em all about it." The more sedate mothers have no such roguish wiles. They tend their jumpy little kids with solicitude and circulate among the males quite unconcerned. Then there are the mannish females, some with rudimentary horns. They act like males, have sham battles and cavort outlandishly at times. They are doubtless a social menace, at least they seem more like officious feminists than anything else. So these neat little creatures, scratching ticks from their ears dexterously with a hind foot, dusting their spotless tan and white coats with dry powdered earth, flicking their nervous little tails incessantly, constitute one of the most interesting and charming pictures of game life. We admire them greatly.

Now the rain has started in earnest and comes down on the thatched roof with a soft rustle and patters on the ground soothingly. Gray clouds roll in overlapping masses of vapor high above us and a low lying veil of mist shrouds the distant hills.

Across the brown plains the barrage of falling water sweeps the withered grass and wakes again the fragrance of the earth.

Before me the camp fire hisses as the drops strike the glowing embers and the smoke weaves back and forth, loath to rise against the downpour. All the camp sounds become subdued, the scene is pervaded by the hush of inspiration. This is the magic of another phase in Nature.

A. THOMSON'S GAZELLE

XXIII

RHINOS BEWARE

July 21st, 1925.

THIS rhino plot thickens! We are getting warm, if such a phrase may be accepted in the tropics. Today I saw fresh rhino tracks down at the river. A big fellow had taken a bath at night and passed within half a mile of our camp.

So far our experience with rhinos has been scant. They are around here, but in small numbers. In fact they are not as numerous anywhere in British East Africa as they used to be. They are destructive to fences and farms and are such fools that they invite extermination. And yet they are dangerous.

The latest story current in Nairobi, as we passed through, was to the effect that some woman sportsman wounded a rhino with a small bore gun. It charged her and her companion, wounding them both, I believe, then disappeared in the brush. The next day a man and his wife were passing through this district in their car, when it stalled in a ditch. As the man got out to crank the car, the rhino, who happened to be standing behind a bush, where of all places in Africa the car happened to stall, charged him, killed him, charged the car, wrecked it, saw the wife, charged and fatally wounded her.

And just after we left Nairobi word came that Captain Ritchie, the game warden, went out to dispatch a troublesome rhino. They met in the bush, the Captain fired; the bullet deflected by a limb only wounded the beast; the rhino charged, bowled Captain Ritchie over, and as he fell caught him with its horn; pushed him along the ground, rolled him up into a heap and ran over him without doing further damage. The Captain gathered himself together, shot the rhino again and killed it.

It seems that it is perfectly possible to dodge a rhino charge if one keeps his presence of mind and is active. The animal has poor vision and lowers his head when near his victim. He governs his attack more by the sense of smell than by sight. Natives say that one can step aside and let a rhino pass.

In olden days when gangs of slaves were taken out of this very country, chained by the neck, one to another, a rhino charging through this line of walking blacks, used to produce untold havoc and death. Imagine such a catastrophe being added to the misery of these unfortunate men. Probably in America today are descendants of slaves taken from Ikoma, our neighboring village, sold by Portuguese traders at prices as low as fifteen dollars apiece, or ten cents a pound for human flesh.

The Masai are said to kill rhino with their spears. As the creature rushes upon them, they side-step his attack, grasp the animal by its erect tail, and, holding to this support, they run and drive their long heavy spears into its flank.

The Wassukuma, or natives of this district, either catch them in pits dug in the pathway, covered with light brush, or shoot them with poisoned arrows. Round about here they have been pretty well exterminated by this method of hunting. It is also reported that they were slaughtered by the Germans at Kilimafeza, a nearby mine, where their hides were used to make buckets for the hoist.

The body of a dead rhino will attract more lions than any known carcass. It seems to have a long distance penetrating odor that no lion can resist. I think Simson said he once counted twelve lions feeding on one dead rhinoceros.

My brother and his hunting companions who had experience with an active member of the species in Kenya, are willing to make an affidavit to the effect that with all this bulk and general appearance of awkwardness, a charging rhino is as quick as a cat and can turn on a twenty-five cent piece. One of this expedition can also attest to it that a rhino can whip about a tree just as fast as a man can circle it. In fact, dodging

187

around a tree seems to be the favorite sport of this particular pachyderm.

In brush country they are considered more dangerous than in fairly open country, for here they bear down upon one and catch him in the clinging thorns and un-yielding undergrowth; which of course is no impediment to a healthy rhinoceros.

Well, in spite of all this we have been after them and expect to go again. It may be that we shall only tickle their short ribs with our arrows, perhaps more than that. It may be that we have to climb a tree post haste and whistle for a rescue party.

You never can tell in Africa.

Our first encounter, you recall, came early in our experience here, and after an attempted stalk in more or less open country, the rhino got a hazy idea that something was wrong and left for parts unknown.

The second contact with this worthy gentleman was likewise on the open plains. "We saw him when he was yet a great way off." We circled miles to get down wind, and watched him at half a mile while he fiddled and fussed and at last lay down to take his noon-day nap.

Sleeping seems to be the best thing he does. So after turning and picking his ground with the utmost deliberation, he at last settled back on his rump and curled his forelegs under his barrel-like body and went off into gentle slumber.

MAKING NATIVE ARROW POISON

It looked gentle from a distance, but to a practiced eye, he has all the earmarks of one who snores. With such a nose, what else could one do to keep it occupied. And while wrapt in gentle slumber the rhino birds hopped over his head and ears and spinal column and picked ticks off his corrugated integument and generally disported themselves. In this happy scene, we drew nearer.

Vague forebodings in his dreams caused him to turn and open an eye; the tick birds soared aloft and twittered. We held still in our crouched position and waited for the troubled dream to pass.

He slept again, and once more we stole cautiously nearer, one right behind the other, and making little motion with the body; all this on the open veldt.

The warning birds arose and scolded. But only a sleepy response came from our stuperous friend. Slowly we crept upon him; seventy yards off and a strong cross wind blowing; too far for effective shooting with our heavy rhino arrows, with their long tempered steel blades; seventy yards and he got a subconscious impression of something important to his future well-being.

He shook off his lethargy and staggered to his feet. I must admit that he is alacritous about arising. He was up and thinking very hard, all in a moment. He stood and thought: "Something is wrong! What is it?"

He turned this way and that, testing the wind. He

gazed fixedly in our direction, but could find little to focus upon there. He was puzzled!

The birds gossiped and fluttered; he shifted nervously, like a fat man ill at ease, in tight trousers, and we were too far off to shoot with a bow. So we took his photograph, profile and front view, we snapped the camera at him. In perplexed and troubled mood, in that haughty superior look he cultivates to cover his vacuity of thought, we snapped them all.

Then, having posed as long as the artists could reasonably ask, he wheeled abruptly and left like a man who had a clear cut purpose in life and bent every energy upon attaining it.

We did not even send a shaft in his direction. I wish we had, just to get the feeling of shooting at a rhino. And we haven't seen him since.

Now Arthur Young has met one, and unavoidably had to give him his quietus with the rifle. I know Art would have let him taste the temper of his steel arrowhead if there had been the slightest chance.

Having hunted so many years with Young and shot all sorts and conditions of game with him, I know that there are none too big nor too fierce for the bow of this hearty lad.

As our other companion in arms, that grand old archer, Will Compton, used to say: "Study your shot: draw to the barb, loose softly and may bright Phoebus guide your shaft!"

So with these footprints on the sands of time, or at least rhino tracks down by the river, Art Young and White returning this week from their side trip, the moon on the wane, the wind from the west, the wild guinea hens roosting high, and a certain feeling in my old bones, I have a "hunch" that something is going to happen, regrettable it is true, but sure to happen to one particular rhino in Tanganyika.

Let him gird up his loins and prepare to meet his manufacturer!

As for me, I am going over to the hut yonder and take out a little carborundum stone and whet up a dozen fine tempered steel rhino heads, six inches long and like daggers, and wax the string on my eighty-pound yew bow. Bloodthirsty is no name for it. It is murder in the first degree!

But wait a bit, you may have a rhino laugh on us yet!

XXIV

EDUCATION OF A WANDOROBO

July 23rd, 1925.

B WANAS WHITE and Young have returned from
their expedition, and incidentally brought in the
pelts of seventeen more lions.

They covered a hitherto unexplored country, found
countless numbers of game of all sorts and thoroughly
enjoyed three weeks or more of tent life. But the
experience which seems to stand out in the strongest
light, was not the lions they brought to bag, but the
visit they had from some genuine wild men. Even for
this wild country, these men by comparison were wilder
yet. They were the real Wandorobo; gypsies of the
African jungle.

At times, members of the various tribes take to the
jungle and live as the Wandorobo, but they remain
essentially typical of their people; while the Simon pure
Wandorobo is born to the land.

You may recall that we saw some natives hunting
wildebeest with the bows, and we surprised them in

their camp, and how they fled. Well, these are the same gang.

White and Young were looking for lions and unexpectedly ran close to these little fellows as they lay in the grass, hiding. They jumped up and started to run away, when the native gunbearer leveled the little 22 rifle at them and called a warning to stop, in Swahili. One of these savages knew a little of this dialect and brought them to a halt. When White and Young came up and asked why they had run away, the linguist of the band explained that they had never seen white men before and they were scared. White told them that no harm would come, so they gratefully said "Bwana Mizuri" —or "good master"—and accepted the bond of faith.

Then they were asked where to find lions and one of them agreed to show. So after considerable doubt he attached himself to the white man's party and went along. Later he explained that the old man of the band had tried to dissuade him from so rash a venture, but he naively stated that he was promised a shilling a lion, would get meat to eat and ride in that wonderful conveyance, the motor car. He could not resist.

Before leaving, however, he did the proper thing and introduced the members of his tribe to the Bwanas. He told his own name, and who his father was: he likewise informed White of the ancestry of three other natives: he had already introduced the "Baba," or father of the band, as the "wise one," and last he called forth the standing army and presented a fine youth, as the "soldiers." He was the "Protector of the Faithful."

One of the Wandorobo had a document with him. Every native of Africa carries with him, or is supposed to, a little aluminum case in which are his identification papers, giving his name, tribe, age, father's name, date of circumcision and other data, as well as his thumb print. This is made out by the District Commissioner, and everyone who employs this native must inscribe upon the paper when and where and how much pay and all things relative to his service. This one lad was the only proud possessor of this sort of document. He fell upon his knees before Bwana White, handed up this potent charm, worn about his neck on a leather thong, and then in a most suppliant manner he rubbed his palms prayerfully together till it was perused and handed back to him. Oh, the power of the written word!

The little fellow who became their guide was not over five feet tall, and more like a quaint little monkey than a man. He had a fragment of grimy cloth about his loins, a bracelet and a bow and arrow. Think of venturing into the heart of Africa with no more to your outfit than that!

When he wanted a fire he twirled one stick on another and had it in a minute. When he wanted

BAITING A BOMA

shelter he crept under a palm plant or in a vacant cave. The caves we had found with the paintings in them were the habitats of these people.

When he wanted food he shot it somehow with his bow. It is strange "how little we mortals need below, nor need that little long!"

So in he climbed on the back seat of the Ford truck and immediately became a part of civilization. Imagine his sensations, having risen in one glorious moment to this position in life! He became the guide: the leader of these mysterious white men. He led them to lions; he saw them shoot, he stayed in the back seat while they raced at the incredible speed of twenty or thirty miles an hour over the veldt after cheeta.

He and his companions saw the white man kill them meat at three hundred yards: saw the beast drop in its tracks, and they all gave that funny exclamation of surprise and admiration, which is half a grunt and half a cough. For as the guide he rode proudly away in the car, the rest followed on a tireless run like a pack of dogs. They laughed with glee to watch the wheels go round. At last they were distanced and went back to their own camp carrying the fresh killed meat, and a new idea.

So the little savage stayed with white men three days, living a life of wondrous adventure. He won his shillings, five of them: he drank in all the marvels of the camp: he picked up every empty cartridge and secreted it as a precious jewel. Nothing was wasted about camp, it all went to "Wandy." And he was to get wages too, at the rate of ten shillings a month. He even learned to lean over the side of the traveling car and keep a look out for punctures. But on the fourth day he was gone, no word, no sound, no note of explanation. He had just departed. Apparently all this wealth had deranged his mind, or perhaps in the wisdom of the jungle he decided that he had better decamp before these rich presents were taken back. It was too good to be true, so he left before the dream exploded.

He was to get arrow heads and salary, and more meat. But the last present Bwana gave him was a set of glass beads costing twenty-five cents at the Emporium, but they stunned him. He held them in his hand and looked away like a puzzled monkey. Neither recognition nor gratitude crossed his features. He held them limply in his hand, then almost slyly he glided away and hid them whence none might recover.

This was the last straw. Prodigality of gifts lost them a leader. But they never will forget funny little "Wandy."

Oh, yes, I must tell you that his eyes nearly fell out when he saw Young's bow and arrows. He tried to pull this mighty weapon, then he solemnly went up to Young and shook him by the hand. He also saw Art shoot a reed buck at seventy yards with the bow, and bring down a flying goose with an arrow. No such archery ever came within his ken before. Perhaps this contributed to his delinquency.

Farewell, little Wandorobo!

Another amusing chapter of their experience was the honor of being chased in their motor car by a rhino. This old pachyderm had routed the natives when they went for water at the pool in the evening. He charged a topi that crossed his line of vision and almost ran down a fleeting hyena who got to the windward of him. So when he saw the Ford he decided here was a rival worthy of his horn. He took after it and doubtless would have demolished the "old boat" had not the captain put on every yard of canvas and ordered full steam ahead. They just made it over the hill a little in advance of the insurgent antedeluvian monster.

Later on Young and White trimmed his corns for him. We have his horns and feet in camp now, the two essential features of the gentleman: the lions got the rest. The morning after, not a bone, not a vestige of that huge beast was left on the veldt.

The longest shot made by any of us with the bow was one by Arthur Young on this recent safari. He hit a gazelle at 155 yards and downed it. Curiously enough, as it dropped, a hyena that was in hiding near by rushed out and seized the gazelle in his jaws and ran off with it. Young started in hot pursuit and chased the hyena who stopped at intervals to eat his capture,

197

then sped off with the body, lay down and tore his prey again. This chase continued for nearly a mile, Young running and shooting as the thief took a quick lunch. Both man and predatory beast were pretty well exhausted when at last Young's arrow grazed the hyena so close that he decided he had enough. In fact he had, for half the "Tommy" was gone. However, Young packed the remains to camp to prove that his adventure was not pure moonshine.

Speaking of rhinos, of course that brings us back to ours, and his probable lease of life. I conjecture that he will live another half century. We sent out native scouts to run him to earth or find his whereabouts, so that some experimental archery might, per adventure, be perpetrated upon him. But he was conspicuous by his absence. And 'tis just as well. We have no time at present to be fooling with a rhino. We are packing our duffle and getting ready to leave for the Grumeti River, where we shall spend another month or so finishing up our bow and arrow crusade, thence on to Nairobi and Mombasa, home.

At the Grumeti we hope to meet other rhino and other adventures. There are plenty of rhino there.

Our own contribution to the archery score in the past few days was the shooting of another antelope with the bow.

The injured gunbearers are improving, and Kysuma will be able to follow the safari on foot. Solomani rides with the camp outfit, all dolled up in his bandages and the green shirt I've given him.

We have distributed many of our arrows and safety razor blades among the Ikoma boys, and they were like gifts from heaven.

I think this year will mark an epoch in their lives: the safari of the white men who shot the bow and arrow will never be forgotten. They know we killed lions and large game like the eland, and the honor and respect with which they hold these feats will live long in their memory.

XXV

AT THE GRUMETI RIVER

August 13th, 1925.

WE arrived here bag and baggage more than a week ago and are camped at a delightful spring of clear running water. They call it Simson's Spring, or as the natives pronounce it: "Campi a *Shim shim.*"

The trophies and most of our camp stuff we sent on ahead by porters, and followed in the two machines later. There was some question whether or not we could make the trip successfully because of the rains which fell in heavy precipitation all about us. But fortune favored us, as she has throughout the expedition, and, meeting with no serious impediments, we accomplished the eighty miles from the Sironera River in one day. The foot safari required nearly a week.

The type of country surrounding us is quite different from that of our previous location. The land is broken up into short valleys and cut by many wooded streams. It presents the character of jungle Africa, especially along the wide river bed which courses through the broken terrain.

Game, which usually is abundant, according to all native reports, is at present very scarce.

We had hoped to do quite a bit of ambush shooting and stalking of the antelope and buck families. Impalla, particularly, should be present in great numbers, browsing on the slopes of the thickly wooded range of hills which runs for several miles west of our camp. They are, however, conspicuously absent, or occupy the open country, contrary to all rules, while the zebra and eland, though few in number, have taken to hill climbing and seek the ridges.

One feature of the camp is very attractive: we are on the edge of rather heavy tropic vegetation, and have in consequence a population of monkeys, sacred ibis, wailing lemurs and other jungle folk that make for good company and amusement. The lemurs particularly are strangely engaging and we hear their weird cry at night, one that resembles nothing so much as a very young baby with the colic. The sacred ibis also has a most uncanny call, coming as it does from the depth of the forest it seems more outlandish and discordant than it ought to be.

High up in the tangled vines of some mango tree this strange bird roosts, then squawks and flies to some sunlit pool beneath drooping limbs and there struts about in a most gawkish manner, so that I, for one, can never imagine why anybody ever thought it *sacred*. It seems only diabolical to me.

Bird life is particularly varied at the water holes and gives one a delightful opportunity to study their actions from a secluded retreat.

Buffalo and rhino also frequent these places. One pool in particular in the deep shadow of the jungle seems to have been a buffalo bathing resort for ages. The worn trails and scarred trees where the brutes have rubbed their horns for generations give evidence of great antiquity.

In the river bed, too, we find recent evidence of these animals. Their migrations seem to be almost entirely at night. In fact, it seems that one old buffalo bull accompanied, or followed, by a rhinoceros companion makes regular night trips past our camp, wallowing in the chain of mud holes that runs down to the river.

The buffalo signs were so thick that Young and I determined to follow them up with an idea of learning their numbers and whereabouts, so that possibly we could try the effect of our flying shafts upon them.

Of course, the African buffalo is an extremely tough and dangerous animal, resourceful and vindictive, so we went prepared for casualties. White left us at this stage and made a flying trip to Nairobi to see to our final arrangements and sailing reservations.

Young assumed the responsibilities of repelling

the impromptu attack from buffalo and rhino, while we threaded these jungle paths. . . . We hardly hoped to be able to shoot either of these great beasts with the bow, still Young always had his archery tackle carried by a native boy, and I tagged around after him with the furtive wish that opportunity might favor us.

The circumstances which would permit us to get within safe bow shot of a rhino or a buffalo we knew must be few and far between, still such opportunities do occur and we sought them always.

Day after day we walked through the endless ramifications of river trails, or climbed the hills where the spoor of both of these beasts lead us. It was a novel thought to me that a heavy pachyderm like a rhino could clamber up mountain ascents and chose by preference the ridge trails and stony outcroppings for his daily exercise. Up here, however, we found their most recent tracks and droppings.

On one certain run way of the summit, where rough rocky ramparts flanked the path, we ran across tracks of a large lion, a rhino and a buffalo, all so recent that we fancied we could detect the animal heat of them, and felt correspondingly cold and uncomfortable up and down the spine, as we crept through the brush of this extremely uninviting trail. Every second we looked for a rush at us from the tangled cover.

It certainly heightens one's sense of perception and

keeps the blood pressure, pulse rate and vasomotor functions at top notch.

Here and in the river bottom we always picked a possible tree, along the line of our march to which we held with our eye as a spot of refuge upon an instant's warning. Thus we advanced from one source of comfort to the next tree. These are the trepidations of the trail. Our native boys also felt the danger, and Young's bow bearer always asked me to string that mighty weapon and he carried it ready with an arrow on the string when crossing a donga.

Baboons leaped from the tall grass and crashed through the branches of fallen trees, so that our hearts popped into our throats. Spur fowl whirred from under our feet and disappeared with a roar like shots from a machine gun. Things of this sort were not conducive to tranquillity.

At some of the buffalo pools, where steep banks and overhanging vegetation acted as screens, we thought we might wait in trees for these wary animals to come and drink, there to try our bows upon them. But the chances of meeting them seemed very poor where so many water holes existed, and it meant midnight vigils, so we continued our wanderings.

We did, of course, see water bucks and a few kongoni, and tried our best to secure specimens with our artillery, but fortune did not favor us.

It rained often during these days, and we sat beneath

AN ARCHER AND TWO JACKALS

the large leaved trees and waited while the storm king overhead drove his hurtling chariot across the heavens and rumbled off over the hill.

There is a dramatic sequence to a tropical storm that charms one into a happy reverie, when no pressing necessities urge him to fretful impatience. One has but to sit and wait awhile, keeping the bow from wet, and the arrows sheltered close to the tree. The downpour arrives all at once and rattles on the leaves, strikes the warm earth with rising clouds of vapor. Birds sit in muffled crouched attitudes in the brush, insect life disappears, and the native porters with us huddle half sheltered from the storm with seeming indifference to the wet. I watch the streams of water run down their statuesque bodies, flow over the rounded contour of their muscles, over the velvet texture of their skin and see the little tremulous quiver of tendons in their legs. They do not mind.

It grows lighter; the mist of rain clears; the rush and forest clatter fades and individual drops are heard to fall. Light breaks through; crystal diadems of sunlight glitter on the green leaves and the storm is over. The birds begin to chirp and sing again.

We rise stiff-legged from our shelter and follow the quest of the elusive buffalo.

We found their retreat, where they hid in the day time. A herd of a dozen or more ranged in our vicinity. We saw them through the glasses at dusk. They were huge, ugly brutes, very quick in action and apparently very keenly sensitive to scent and sound. The presence of swarms of buffalo gnats told us of their proximity. We could even detect their odor. It was like the familiar fragrance of domestic cattle.

We met them, too, but not when we wanted to, and certainly in no position suitable for an archer. While circling a large clump of dense bush in search of our quarry, suddenly two buffalo cows dashed out of the cover and ran straight for us. Their approach had all the appearance of an unprovoked charge, but in the very instant that we sprang together for defense, they swerved and rushed past us, but not in time to save themselves by their change of tactics, for Young fired two shots so rapidly at the foremost female that hardly two jumps occurred between them. Both bullets struck in the buffalo's shoulder, and she and her companion rushed off into the river bottom, where we heard the wounded one fall and groan her last.

It was all over in a few seconds, and we hardly realized our danger before the rush; the shots; the dying beast lay on its side in the tall grass of the donga. I had little time to string a bow, less time to draw a shaft and less presence of mind to do either, than you fancy.

It was not a bowman's occasion, and still we hunted, hoping for that rare chance that might come.

Just at evening, a day or so later, as Young and his

small party were coming through a clear space on the hill side, a huge bull took after a native in the rear and drove pell mell for him. At the first yell of the frightened boy, Young turned and saw the native running like a sprinter, his chest out, his rapidly moving knees drawn up in front of him with each stride and emitting an agonized cry. The buffalo came on, his head lowered, lunging nearer and nearer the black. With phenomenal quickness and accuracy Young fired three shots into the bull's foreshoulder at twenty paces, with his Winchester 30–06–rifle, and tumbled the old beast on his nose. The gun bearers say that "Bwana Yangi" (Young) is the best rifle shot they have ever seen.

Here again was no situation for an archer. But our hour did arrive, and to show you how poorly we met it, I will continue the story. It is a tale of defeat, but only one of the many discouragements that must fall to the lot of all hunters. We can not always win; in fact, in this land, we count ourselves fortunate if we come off with honors even and no scratches.

We met our rhino. There were several rambling about, but they all seemed to be nocturnal, and in consequence we did not run into each other, since Africa is not a healthy place for midnight walks.

This day we had climbed a steep ridge back of the buffalo forest. The slope was deep in grasses, fragrant mint and a succulent herb that looked like smilax. This seemed to be the favorite food of these ruminants.

We had reached the summit and sat down to search the plain below with our glasses, when out from the forest shade ambled a rhino, apparently travelling due north in haste. He was a moderate sized individual and very active. I was surprised at his gait. In a brief space of time he had crossed the half mile of level ground and begun the ascent of our hill.

Once or twice he seemed to get our scent, or our trail off the ground, and stopped to think, looking from side to side, then went on. He came straight for us as we sat poorly screened on the side hill. We believed he could not see us, but chance seemed to direct his course unerringly.

As he reached the steep gradient of the hills, I was astonished to see the beast, not only fail to slacken his pace, but actually increase it. He mounted that rise with all the light footed delicacy of a cattle pony.

He seemed so determined to run over our position, that as he passed through a patch of brush, we quickly shifted our station and concealed ourselves in a small clump of trees. The rhino came right up to our level, then disappeared in the scrub jungle of a nearby eminence. He did not emerge, so we crept up the crest to leeward and tried to locate him in the cover.

Soon we saw him, motionless and obscure, behind some small trees, forty yards off. Young and I had our bows braced and the large rhino arrows nocked on the string. But there was no opportunity to shoot;

the intervening limbs spoiled our chances to strike home.

Suddenly the rhino got the notion that this was not a wholesome place to rest and turned rapidly and dove into the thicker brush.

As he wheeled and exposed his broadside, I let fly an arrow at his flank. It was aimed at the small triangular area between the hip and the last rib. Here I decided was the best anatomical spot for an entrance wound with an arrow. Alas! I did not hit it. My alibi is that I was shooting down a steep declivity, my arrow was unusually heavy and I underestimated the distance. The shot went six inches below the belly line and struck the rocky ground beneath him. The rhino disappeared in the jungle.

Young did not shoot, through a false sense of hunting courtesy. I wish he had. He might have hit the rhino I missed.

Some very good authorities have said that it is impossible to kill a rhinoceros with the bow and arrow without the use of poison, and we have been discouraged from even trying it. But to an archer this is only a challenge. We wished to try the experiment. Every large beast that we have conquered with the bow, such as the moose, the lion, the grizzly and kadiak bear, has been held to be invincible, until we proved that after all they are only flesh and blood.

In the South Kensington Museum are the illustrations to Abul Fazl's "Life of Akbar." In these it is shown that the rhinoceros was killed with a bow and arrow.

Alan Black, one of the "old school" African hunters, a contemporary of Selous and Cunninghame, has said that there is no doubt in his mind that an arrow will kill a rhino, if properly placed. He has driven his hunting knife into the heart, and he admits that a flank shot is an easy entrance to a very vital area, which ultimately must produce death of the beast.

He himself shot one with a poisoned arrow and dispatched it.

So we believe we can slay a rhino with our old English bow and clean broad head arrows.

If we don't do it, some one else will.

XXVI

THE LAST LION

August 18th, 1925.

OUR head man, Mdolo, is boiling the leg bones of Art's buffalo to make soup. He has added the bark of a certain tree to the concoction, a very special sort of bark, and the finished drink, he tells me, is a sure cure for rheumatism; weak knees; old age and general debility. Marvelous soup! We need it!

I was greatly interested in the device he used in cooling the broth. It was a slender stick on the end of which were bound two cross limbs, an inch or more in length. This implement he held between the palms and twirled in such a manner that the hot liquid was thrown into a state of agitation with a rapid dissipation of heat.

All of our trophies; hides, skulls and horns, are being packed and made ready for our departure. The major part of the camp supplies we turned over to Mr. Harrison, a fellow American, who came through our territory with Percival, the white hunter, on his way to the Sironera last week.

Our stay here has been very pleasant. The boys have constructed many grass huts; the setting is most delightful and the weather is all that could be desired. Rains have fallen, but they have not deterred us from hunting. We plan to leave in a few days and return to Nairobi.

One feature of the land that has been of great interest to me is the presence of the uchungo tree, from which the native arrow poison is made. It grows along the river. Often when walking through the forest, I have caught the most heavenly fragrance. It reminded me of jasmine or daphne in elegance, but look as I would on the ground, or in the grass about me, no flower or shrub could I find that gave forth that delicious odor. At last one day I glanced overhead and saw clusters of minute white flowers in the tree above. The leaves of the tree were a dark, glossy green, oval in shape, about an inch long. The bark was gray and fuzzy; the whole tree not more than twenty feet high, and looked something like a myrtle. The native boy with me said it was "uchungo," and that he knew how to make the poison. His tribe came many miles to this river to get the wood.

So I contracted with him to make me a quantity of this toxic substance. He did so. First he chopped a portion of the wood into pieces hardly larger than matches. He boiled a great quantity of these in a gasoline can filled with water. After all day simmering, he took out the wood, leaving a couple of quarts of thick black liquid in the utensil.

Next day he evaporated this slowly in a piece of a broken pot, resting on stones above a bed of coals. After hours of careful stirring and fanning, there remained a tar-like residue, about a pint in quantity, which when cooled was placed in a section of bamboo and presented to me as the finished poison.

Later I learned that this tree has the botanical name —*Acocanthea Schimperi.*

The poison I shall have tested in the department of physiology at the University of California.

We have a number of African arrows and bows, which we are shipping out with our trophies. They were gifts from the Sultani of Ikoma. But we still use the old English bow and broad head arrow,—clean and sharp for the chase.

In the past week we have continued our study of the game problem. One thing that seemed to be established is that African game is almost too wary to be hit with an arrow.

In fact, all the animals seem to be nervous wrecks in Africa and always have the jumps. Their life seems to be one continuous attack of convulsion. They can jump out of a sound sleep and be at top speed before they open an eye to see what tried to get them. Young and I have used less than one hundred arrows apiece though some of these were shot several times. Our accuracy during the entire trip has been below standard.

In spite of all this, we have killed enough game with the bow to have kept us in meat for our personal use. I do not say that we depended upon the bow, but our bag, properly conserved, would have been ample for a party of four.

Fully three quarters of our time was devoted to lion hunting, to the neglect of other game shooting, but notwithstanding this preoccupation, we shot 2 eland, 3 wildebeest, 1 kongoni, 1 water buck, 3 reed buck, 6 Thompson's gazelles, besides such small game as geese, guinea hens, rabbits, hyrax and such other inedible animals as foxes, jackals, hyenas, badgers and baboons.

A single wildebeest would last our party a couple of weeks, using dried meat as food, so we really had more than we needed.

While it is true that game will dodge an arrow, I found by experiment that when I shot at a distance of fifty or sixty yards, and shot over a bush or tall grass, so that the bowman and initial flight of the arrow were hidden, I could strike without first alarming our quarry. They did not see the arrow in flight. We could also shoot from dongas or dry water courses and hit before we were discovered.

Padding the bow with flannel cloth where the arrow crosses the handle, thus making the shot almost silent, also helped us to secure our game.

Of course, the archer must keep off the skyline, if he wants to approach game. Only one thing in Africa seems to cause more alarm to the animal population than an erect biped, and that is a pack of wild dogs.

We have seen game go streaming off the landscape, apparently a mile in advance of some object of excitement, to find later that their terror was caused by a group of wild dogs scouting the veldt. They are the most ruthless and persistent destroyers of game in the country. Even lions leave where they hunt.

The lion is not really afraid; he just naturally detests a dog.

Contrary to what one might expect, the king of beasts himself causes only a local commotion, in the day time, and game moves out of his way but a short distance, then returns to the main business of life,—feeding.

Speaking of lions, we have just shot, probably, our last and best specimen of Felis Leo.

No matter how many lions we shoot with the bow, somebody is always taking the joy out of the jungle by saying, "Yes, but you couldn't do it without being backed up by the big boys with the guns!"

Yes, we could! There are several lions on our list that we met in the tall grass that could have been shot safely with the bow and no gun about.

We were led into this lion game by riflemen and required to fill the order according to their specification. And we did that! But we made a mistake in going

215

with them at all, as nice as they are. We should have gone at the whole hunt like archers, using stalking and ambush instead of rushing out in the open and challenging our lions and provoking attack. But the best lion in our bag we got without "benefit of clergy"; "the man behind the gun." We have also answered the questions: "How many arrows does it take to kill a lion?" "How long does it take him to die?"

At the Grumeti we discovered an old blind, built a year or more past by Leslie Simson. It was near a very rugged mountain and a good stream of water. Game was scarce thereabouts and lion signs plentiful.

Simson and White have both repeatedly stated that though they did not consider boma shooting first class sport, they did thoroughly approve of this method of hunting lions with the bow. Besides these, it has received the approval of such English sportsmen as Leslie Tarlton and Phillip Percival.

So Young and I decided to place a bait at this boma and try for one more lion. We shot a kongoni and dragged him over the country behind the car and ended our circuit by tying him to a tree some fifteen yards in front of the blind.

The thorns of this brush shelter were old and rotten and few and far between, but they looked like protection, even if they were really weak and too porous. A lion could leap through it if he wanted to, or over it.

The first night we simply covered our bait with

brush, to keep off the hyenas and vultures, and stayed in camp. In the morning, our inspection showed that a lion had eaten part of the kongoni and left his shockingly large footprints at the stream bank, where he drank after supper.

So we prepared to sit up with him the next night and went early to the boma, a spot two miles from camp.

Sitting in a clump of thin, rotten thorns, waiting for a lion to come up and mess about you, is an emotional novelty act. You sit there holding your breath, hoping that he does come, and fingering your arrow heads and bow string, wondering if you have done the right thing in leaving your nice warm bed and crawling into this miserable bunch of little sticks, so close to him.

The sun went down; a cool breeze drifted across the land; the bats began to fly about; an owl hooted in the distance, and we sat down on the sweet jungle grass in the blind and waited.

But he did not keep us waiting long. That was a blessing. The moon was about full and rose over the hill. Dusk settled on the land and the shadow of the mountain lay gloomy before us, when down wind, on the trail of our drag, we heard the grunt of a lion, no sound from his feet. He came in fast and had not smelled us. As he neared the bait he gave a great sigh of satisfaction, and made a clucking noise in his throat.

We listened to all this as we lay well back in the

217

corner of the boma, hardly daring to breathe. Then he fell upon the carcass and lapping, licking, tearing and gulping sounds came to our ears.

Noiselessly, and with infinite caution, Art Young rose to the window in the blind and studied the crouching form in the dim moonlight beneath the tree. He motioned to me; I peered out and saw what I thought to be his dark mane and outstretched body lying broadside to us. We braced our bows; nocked our arrows, and settled ourselves to shoot. At a whispered count, we let fly.

There was a grunting roar and in one bound the lion stood before the aperture in our blind, his mane standing erect, glaring at us with green eyes like two X-ray tubes. He was so near I could have touched him with my bow. I saw the shadowed outline of a feathered shaft deep in his side.

It was but the flash of a picture; bristling with rage, towering magnificently before us in the dim illumination, he saw us as we dodged below the opening in the blind. I thought he was about to leap through our scant shelter and strike us dead. He was a tremendous beast. But something misgave him. Either he felt his mortal wound, or the arrow diverted him, or he sought a better position for attack. At any rate, he whirled and galloped off before our boma, but hidden by the trees. We heard the blood rattle in his throat as he went. We heard him fall and crash the arrow

ARTHUR YOUNG AND HIS TROPHY

shaft in his teeth; we heard him give a long low moan, and all was quiet.

The moon crossed the firmament; a leopard coughed in the donga; hyenas wailed on the veldt. Night is long in Africa.

The weary hours passed at last, hours when we dare not venture from our shelter. The stars grew pale; the dawn bird called from the thorn tree. Then in the gray morning light, we crawled out of the boma and walked up to our lion. There he lay facing us, fallen forward, but ready to meet his enemy. Sixty-nine yards from the boma he lay. The soft wind which blows before sunrise tossed his great mane gently to and fro. He lay as if asleep and we drew near him with caution and awe, casting little clods of earth at his still form before venturing to touch him.

Young's arrow, buried to the feather, transfixed him through the chest, above the heart. It had severed his pulmonary artery, cut two ribs and protruded through the opposite side of the body.

After being hit he had not lived 15 seconds. One arrow killed him.

There lay the finest maned lion in Africa killed with the bow and arrow. It was a wonderful sight!

I grasped the hand of Arthur Young over the body of this fallen monarch, the greatest trophy of our long years of shooting together.

There are many disappointments and discouraging

circumstances of the chase, especially to an archer but our comradeship and admiration has withstood these galling tests. In such moments as this the triumph is not only that of the hunter over the beast, but one of enduring friendship.

XXVII

AN EPILOGUE IN NAIROBI

August 25th, 1925.

HERE we are back where we started five months ago. We arrived in Nairobi after a two day run by automobile from the Grumeti. At Guaso Nyero we paid off our porters and had our trophies shipped by ox team to the railroad. These will be sent by freight to America.

Old Solomani, the wounded gun bearer, we have placed in the care of a local physician. He is, of course, crippled permanently in his right arm, has lost one eye with a portion of his face and is greatly shattered in health. His wife came up from Mombasa and cared for him in a most affectionate and understanding way.

White has provided him with a small pension for life, adequate for his needs, and he goes to the farm of P. H. Percival, where he can have a permanent home. His son, an intelligent lad of eighteen years, has taken up his father's vocation and went out on his first safari soon after our arrival.

We said goodby to Solomani and sent him away with

many presents and our blessing. He is a brave, faithful Swahili.

Because our expedition was one of the novelties of Kenya, we were invited to an informal luncheon at the Government House. Here we met the representative men of the colony. There are no finer type of gentlemen in the world than these British of Kenya.

Young and I were called upon to show our archery tackle and demonstrate how we shoot. It was an interesting event wherein we Americans, descendants from the great Anglo-Saxon race, showed these Englishmen how their ancestors shot the long bow a thousand years ago. I think we gained their approval of our sportsmanship and methods of hunting.

In the days that have followed, many old friends have called upon White to renew congenial contacts of ten years past. Among these not the least pleasant were the visits from native gun bearers and head men of other safaris. Many were the reminiscences and wise observations concerning the superior merits of ye ancient customs and the decadence of the modern days.

Alan Black, a notable hunter of elephants and other big game, called upon us, with his companion, Mr. Judd, who accompanied Roosevelt. Black is a man of very positive opinions and much wisdom. He is the last of the famous old triumvirate with Selous and Cunninghame.

Alan Black was greatly interested in our adventure

because he has imagination and a profound sense of the romantic. But he did not compliment us. He does not do that sort of thing often, but he criticised us very candidly. He said; "When I heard that you had come here with the idea of shooting big game with the bow and arrow, I was glad and admired your nerve. It is true sport. But when I heard that you chased lions in a motor car and were backed up by guns, I was very much disappointed. It was an anachronism and a failure in sportsmanship.

"You should have abandoned all modern resources and gone at the business of stalking and shooting on a purely primitive basis, one compatible with the bow. You should have gone 'native style.'"

Much as it hurts to admit our defeat, I had to concur in his opinion. As archers, we have failed and only by comparison have we any measure of success.

As for shooting rhino and elephant with the bow, he was firmly convinced it could be done. So enthusiastic was he about it that I gave him my eighty-five pound lemon wood bow and a couple of dozen arrows in a quiver, and asked him to continue the experiment. He accepted the offer gladly and assured me that there would be little doubt about killing a rhino on his next hunt. He has shot the native bows and like all good Britons, is a natural archer. So I expect a report of his accomplishment some day.

Not only is Black going to try for rhino, but another

Englishman, Mr. Rodney Wood, who lives in Nyasa-
land, is going on a prolonged expedition, using the bow.
I left him an osage bow and several dozen broad head
arrows, as well as some of our "rhino heads," for his
equipment. So I feel that even if we have failed in the
full measure of our possibilities, others will carry on
the adventure.

Among the unfinished business of our safari is the
report of my comparative anatomical studies made on
the specimens of our hunt.

I did one hundred and ten post mortem examinations
on some twenty-six species of wild game, recording in
particular the anatomy of the biliary system. These
notes, measurements and sketches must be compiled
and sent to the Mayo Clinic. This I expect to do on
board ship during our homeward voyage.

We have come through our experience without serious
illness or mishap, and for this good fortune we have
the gods to thank. We are all well and in possession
of our own hides.

For the successful management of our safari, we have
Stewart Edward White to thank; to Leslie Simson and
to him we are under obligation for their invaluable
services on the firing line. That part of our experiment would have been impossible without them.

We herewith express our gratitude.

I am writing on the porch of the old Norfolk Hotel,
where so many distinguished hunters have gathered in

the bygone days, where the pepper trees planted by Theodore Roosevelt and the Duke of Connaught cast their shade. I sit and watch the life of this little community flow past.

Half clad natives, fresh from the outer zones of barbarism come trotting into town, wide-eyed and timorous, as they view for the first time the marvels of the white man's city. Their more sophisticated brothers parade up and down the thoroughfares arrayed in the fantastic habiliments of European culture and betray the black man's love of gaudy color and incongruous effects. Woolen aviator caps, such as people wear in very cold climates when they go tobogganing or skating, are all the style here in the tropics among the natives. Silk shirts and short khaki trousers are becoming to their graceful bodies. Golf stockings and patent leather slippers complete the picture. Just one more touch is needed, and this is lent by the jaunty little bamboo canes which the dandies carry. Three months out of the jungle and they are finished products of modern culture. But they are very happy in their gay plumage!

Much of the white population seems to be of the languid British type, riding in jinrickshas, if they are women, or popping past on motor cycles, if young men. They never seem to walk.

Automobiles are in abundance; primitive carts drawn by long horned oxen creak slowly up the road, ladened

225

with freight. A fine cloud of golden dust shimmers in the morning sun. Troops of native boys, scantily attired, play a game of soccer, using a small tennis ball which they kick about most dexterously. The King's African Rifles, native soldiers in "shorts" and red fez caps, make a picturesque addition to the scene. The clear vibrant note of a bugle rings out on the velvet air.

This growing metropolis of some five thousand whites and uncountable blacks, with its British type of municipal buildings; its corrugated iron shacks in the Indian quarter, its charming English country homes; its dirt roads lined by eucalyptus trees; its garden walls overgrown with purple bougainvillea, I wonder how long it will stand as an outpost of European civilization?

In a thousand years will Nairobi be a large center of Caucasian life in Africa? Or will the jungle have grown over the ruins and only the black man hear the wail of the hyena on the hills. Who knows?

Our safari is over! Our goods and chattels are packed and ready to go. The little railroad will jiggle us down the escarpment those four hundred or so miles to Mombasa, our trophies will follow us, left to the careful supervision of Safari-land Limited, that firm, under the management of Leslie Tarlton and Col. Whetham, which has so graciously and efficiently handled our safari affairs during our stay. We will climb in the ship which takes us up the Indian Ocean,

LIGHT AND SHADE IN KENYA

through the Red Sea and the Suez Canal and sailing in the blue water of the Mediterranean land us at Genoa, Italy, where we transfer to an American vessel, and after many leagues on water and land, arrive back in California, eight months from the time we left home.

The question that naturally arises now, in some minds, is: "Why did you go to Africa?"

This world being filled with all sorts and conditions of people, it is not strange that some will think we should have stayed at home and attended to our business. Others will hold that all sport is folly and that we should have been at the spiritual labor of improving our souls, singing praises to the Lord and doing works of charity; some there are that hold all men guilty of crime, who take animal life, and consequently we are arch fiends to venture thus into the highways and by-ways seeking what we might slay. But thank goodness! the great majority of men, those who wear pants and use a razor, they know why we went hunting and envy us our lot. But why we went with the bow and arrow, that puzzles the best of them.

Why not take advantage of the perfection of modern firearms, and go at the business like a real man?

Well, now, that's the question I will answer:

We can all shoot a gun; all these men who constitute this expedition, namely: Stewart Edward White, Arthur Young and Saxton Pope, the scribe. I am not a good shot, but we can all pull a trigger and hold a bead.

We have all handled guns since we were knee high to the proverbial grasshopper, and had a lot of fun doing it.

But with varying degrees of perception, we all feel that most hunting with the rifle, in expert hands, lacks the full measure of sport. The advantage is too much in favor of the gunman; too little on the side of the game. For some, this means no more hunting. These men eke out a meagre delight in taking pictures and watching game. This is very laudable and of great profit, but it is only a stepsister to hunting. You can hunt and do this too, especially if you step down your destructive efficiency and accept more equal terms with the game.

In the bow you do this and you add a thrill of romance to your sport when you do it.

Man never had a more perfect weapon than the bow and arrow, from the standpoint of charm and intimate response. The bow becomes part of his mood; member of his faculties, yielding service and direct action in proportion to the throbbing life placed in it. The very sinews of the huntsman are implicated in his weapon. The poise and nicety of his mental state is made manifest in the flight of his arrow. The serenity and steadfast nature of his nerves are registered in its true flight.

The bow is part of the man, and when by painful effort he has conquered its untamed spirit, it becomes a companion in the field and woods, a light burden when he climbs the winding trails, a prop and a stay as he runs and risks a limb, a protector against harmful beasts, sweet company in camp when he tends its simple wants with wax for the string and oil for the timber. He gives it soft shelter from inclement weather, and at night it lies by his side, when both may rest from the chase.

Every arrow in his quiver is a messenger, blithe and gay, singing as it goes, keen in service, when well sped, striking home and slaying humanely and cleanly. When careless prompting from its master lets it wander from the mark, there you will find it calling in the grass where its bright colors send an appeal to your questing eye. Back it goes with its fellows, ever a cheerful philosopher and optimist: "better luck next time!" it murmurs softly as it rustles in the quiver. And all your marks need not be living things. Your shafts are ever ready to leap forth in flight. There is no noise or smoke, no waste or harm. Shoot at yonder dandelion and sink your arrow in the sweet grass. On all sides are little targets for your aim. Cautiously you view the field, then pick out a pine cone on the waving tree top. That is a good mark: now shy an arrow at that and see it fly swift and close, then circle slowly in the air and with perfect grace wing its way home to Mother earth. No harm in that!

Or there squawks a naughty jay, and just to chide him, and hardly hoping to hit him, you loose an arrow at the rascal. A close miss is better than a hit, and off he flies confounded by your magic.

So the day is none too long for the archer. And when he really wants to slay and to capture his quarry, he can do it with the bow. It is no puerile toy, but a man's weapon, honored by our ancestors and worthy of respect today. To prove this, that's why we came to Africa.

For myself I would rather some other disciple of Toxophilus had taken the burden of this African adventure. I do not like to travel these long irksome miles. The sweet forests and purple mountains of California give me all I want in sport. The bounding deer, the panther, the lumbering bear, all are meat for my shafts and those of the hearty lads who have fared with me into the greenwood: Will Compton, Arthur Young, Cassius Styles, Donnan Smith, John Graves, Keith Evans, Monte the Indian, and many another worthy archer.

But here in Africa was the challenge to our beloved weapon, and those who looked askance at our archaic folly, forever held African big game up as a defiance. Here they said, "where they grow them big and fierce, come and try the temper of your broadheads and the cast of your yew, on these beasts!" So we left our gentle pursuits and journeyed twelve thousand miles to answer this challenge to the bow.

We have not slain every sort of beast in this vast domain, but we sought the master of them all, and entered the lists against him. You know how we have borne our honors.

An analysis of our lion statistics is as follows: Five lions were killed by the bow and arrow, absolutely untouched by bullets.

Four lions were mortally wounded by our arrows and would have died if left alone, but through mistake or for humane reasons they were dispatched with the gun; none of these animals charged.

Two lions were mortally wounded with arrows, charged, and were shot with the rifle.

Three lions were slightly wounded and charged our party. They were killed with rifles.

Seven lions charged us while being approached, or having been shot at with arrows, but not hit. These were dispatched with bullets.

In all we had twenty-one encounters. Three lions that we were at first inclined to count as killed by arrows, though they had been unnecessarily shot with the gun, have later been cancelled from our list of conquests, to avoid all question or quibble. The five trophies of the bow are absolutely beyond all cavil or dispute.

We hereby claim five lions to the credit of the bow and arrow.

I cannot say that we have fulfilled the last demand of a perfect contest. We have not bearded the lion in his den, armed only with the bow. That is a possible thing to achieve, but it is no longer sport, it is the ultimate conflict between man and beast; a life for a life, and I judge the odds to be even. That alone is fair play, but it is not sport; it is fierce desperation, too near the primitive to be tolerable.

By the same token, we do not recommend the bow as a proper weapon with which to go lion hunting; no, it is dangerous enough when one uses a gun. But we have shown our weapons adequate to slay, and we contend that with the simple addition to our arms of the spear and shield, we would ask no other protection. Circumstances beyond our control prevented us conducting this experiment. But the assumption is plainly a fair one.

We have conquered the lion, not once by chance, but again and again. Other lesser beasts we met, you may recall: the eland, the wildebeest, the topi, the kongoni, the waterbuck, the reed buck, the gazelles, the hyenas, badgers, foxes, jackals and other smaller fry; these all have capitulated to the bow.

Now what say you, have we not done enough to answer the challenge? May we not now return to the delectable mountains of our native land, where the pine and the oak cast shadows on the carpet of the woods, where sweet water flows, where the deer draw down the dale; the hare scuttles 'neath the bush, and where the meadow lark pipes his mellow note? Such a land suits the bowman, and nature planned this sylvan background for his especial implements of the chase. There with horn and hound and a stout yew stave, no man would seek other fields to conquer.

If you can hear this call, down the avenues of time; if you can smell the dank forest incense and your hand itches to draw a cloth yard shaft across a sturdy bow, then you are one of the immortals. In you we have the heart of the true archer.

To you, I hereby bequeath all the yew trees of this good green earth, that bow staves may be ever yours. I bequeath all stiff wood for arrow shafts and keen steel heads to fit.

Flax and feathers are yours by right of heritage and I leave you, so long as you draw a bow string, all this world of forest and open fields for your delight, and all the wild life therein. And I leave you the sun by day and the moon and stars by night, and the gentle breeze that blows the fragrance of flower and tree and dust to your nostrils.

The long delicious trails and mountain paths are yours. The ecstasy of cool running streams I give you freely when athirst, and last of all I leave to you the thrill of life and the joy of youth that throbs a moment in a well bent bow, then leaps forth in the flight of an arrow.

Saxton Pope —